Ethel Todd Gones

Instructor Professor of
Introduction or Art & Northern
Ren. part at Car WR. for M.A.

James Rosser Johnson

Dean

School of Fine Arts

University of Connecticut

Storrs

THE RADIANCE
OF CHARTRES

*Studies in the early stained glass
of the Cathedral*

by James Rosser Johnson

*Columbia University Studies in
Art History and Archaeology*

Number 4

Random House / New York

TO MY *Mother* AND *Father*

CONTENTS

	List of Illustrations	ix
	Preface	xi
	Introduction	3
I	On Seeing the Windows	7
II	The Stained Glass Theories of Viollet-le-Duc	26
III	The Glass	53
IV	Color Choice and Composition	67
	Notes	82
	Bibliography	91
	Index	95

ILLUSTRATIONS

page 31
> Diagram (from Viollet-le-Duc,
> *Vitrail*, p. 379)

page 38
> Drawings of Head from Saint-Rémi,
> Reims (from Viollet-le-Duc,
> *Vitrail*, pp. 421, 422)

between pages 68 *and* 69

1   *Madonna and Child.* Central Window, West Façade.
    XII century

2   *The Annunciation.* Central Window, West Façade.
    XII century

3   *The Presentation in the Temple.* Central Window,
    West Façade. XII century

4   *The Glorification of the Virgin.* Central Window,
    West Façade. XII century

5   *La Belle Verrière.* South Ambulatory. XII century
    (Photo Houvet, rep. int.)

6   Microphotograph: 5 mm. edge of modern 'lined'
    red glass

7   Microphotograph: 3 mm. edge of Chartres 'flashed'
    red glass, XII century

8   Microphotograph of artificial ruby
    (from Escard, *Les pierres précieuses*,
    Plate XXIII (Fig. 4))

9 Microphotograph of weathered side
   of Chartres XIII century red glass
   showing coating and light streaks

10 A Scene from the Life of St. Ambrose. Altar,
    Milan Cathedral. IX century

11 *The Nativity.* Central Window, West Façade.
    XII century

12 *The Massacre of the Innocents.* Central Window,
    West Façade. XII century

13 *The Three Magi.* Central Window, West Façade.
    XII century

14 *The Annunciation to the Shepherds.* Central Window,
    West Façade. XII century

PREFACE

I AM indebted to the following individuals who have contributed, either directly or indirectly, to the preparation of this work. First of all, I wish to express my gratitude to my wife, who has been a constant source of encouragement and happiness, often at times when my own spirits flagged.

To the late Professor Wilhelm Koehler I shall always be grateful, for it was in his classes at Harvard University that I first became interested in medieval art, and especially in the Cathedral of Chartres. Professor Koehler frequently startled art history students of his day by restricting an entire session to one or two works of art, unhurriedly contemplated, thoughtfully discussed, and brilliantly analyzed. It was here that I began to look.

At the close of the Second World War, I visited Chartres for the first time, spending many memorable hours with its sculpture and glass in the company of Étienne Houvet, beloved guardian of the Cathedral, who was then a very old man. It has always seemed to me that M. Houvet absorbed into his being some of the nobility and serenity of the art of the Cathedral he knew so well. His role at Chartres has happily been continued by his daughter, Mlle. Houvet, who has also been most helpful during my subsequent studies there.

The late and much lamented Jean Maunoury, *Architect-en-chef du Département, Eure et Loir*, was a valued and generous friend, and one of France's most charming ambassadors to America, where he lectured frequently. I am particularly grateful to M. Maunoury for making it possible for me to build scaffolds on the interior of the cathedral to photograph the twelfth-century windows of the west façade. During this time, Mrs. Ruth Jennings Terrill of The Metropolitan Museum of Art was also an inspiring and helpful friend.

The material gathered at Chartres became the subject for my doctoral dissertation at Columbia University, begun under the gracious encouragement of Professor Emerson Swift, and then completed under Professor Meyer Schapiro. Working under the direction of Professor Schapiro is an experience for the graduate student awesome at the beginning, then exasperating, and, in the end, infinitely rewarding. Along with many of his pupils, I am deeply indebted to his leadership and inspiration. Often I have reflected that without Professor Schapiro's counsel and Professor Erwin Panofsky's books, my researches would have been much less rewarding.

Chapters II and III have appeared in the *Art Bulletin*, XLV, 2, June 1963; XXXVIII,3, Sept. 1956 and XXXIX,3, Sept. 1957. They are here reprinted by courtesy of the editors.

Through the generosity of The Cleveland Museum of Art, its Director, Sherman E. Lee, and its Board of Trustees, I received a travel grant in 1961 to return to Chartres and other stained glass centers to make additional observations prior to the completion of this book. I am very grateful for this opportunity. My thanks are also due to Professor Rudolf Wittkower, editor of this series, and to Professor Robert Branner and Professor Howard Davis, for their many helpful suggestions in the final preparation of the manuscript.

Mr. James J. Rorimer and Mr. William Forsyth of The Metropolitan Museum of Art have generously provided access to original material in their medieval collections, and through the courtesy of Mr. Paul Norman Perrot of the Corning Glass Museum I have been able to inspect many examples of antique and medieval glass in that excellent collection.

My appreciation is also extended to Mr. James Grote Van Derpool and Mr. Adolph Placzek of the Avery Library, and to Miss Mary Chamberlin of the Fine Arts Library, Columbia University, for their knowledgeable cooperation. Professor Herschel Chipp was instrumental in making available to me the resources of the University of California Library at Berkeley during an idyllic stay there in the summer of 1956. And thanks are due to Miss Etta Arntzen, who assisted in the editing of the manuscript. Mrs. Alice Wright, Mrs. Eleanor Maher, Mrs. Catherine Sinnott and Miss Dolores Filak of The Cleveland Museum of Art have contributed expert stenographic assistance. To all, my appreciation.

J. R. J.

The Cleveland Museum of Art

THE RADIANCE
OF CHARTRES

Studies in the Early Stained Glass
of the Cathedral

INTRODUCTION

In architectural interest and wealth of sculpture, other Gothic structures may approach the Cathedral of Chartres, but the uniqueness of Chartres resides in its windows. These vast expanses of translucent color have transformed walls and reordered all elements of the interior, never failing to create a deep impression upon the spectator. Cited above all other monuments as the leading center for the study of early Gothic windows, this cathedral has retained, with few exceptions, its full complement of twelfth- and thirteenth-century glass. Few structures have been so fortunate. As if by a miracle, the treasures of Chartres have escaped many of the destructive actions of man and nature which have fallen so tragically upon other cathedrals of comparable age.

The radiance of Chartres is created by these extraordinary windows, masterpieces of an art which during the twelfth and thirteenth centuries became a dominant element in religious architecture, replacing wall frescoes of the Romanesque period. Appropriating the didactic and decorative functions of earlier wall painting, the Gothic stained glass window added an entirely new note by providing its own light source, and establishing the visual condition in which it, as well as all other elements of the interior, were seen. The stained glass artist, working in close collaboration with the cathedral architect and the clergy, could now fashion and control light in a manner consonant with the desired effect of the building: its function, its larger meaning, its ceremonies, and its aesthetic.

Reinforced by religious belief and symbolical association, the Gothic stained glass window was another instance during the Middle Ages of an overwhelming enthusiasm for objects of light and color: gold and silver chalices and altar frontals glittering with polished and embossed surfaces, enamelled reliquaries, richly embroidered cloths and tapestries, sacred book covers glowing with pearls and precious stones, all seen against a background of gilded and painted architecture profusely decorated with sculpture and all manner of fantastic

3

forms. The stained glass window was a monumental expression of this widespread taste for light and color which reached its climax during the Gothic period.

Deriving from the medieval Latin *radiantia*, meaning brightness and splendor, the word radiance is also related to the old French *raie* found often in twelfth-century *chansons de geste* in hymns of praise to the Virgin, describing her bright countenance and her glistening crown of precious stones and gems:

> *Et resplendissent com la raie*
> *Qui en este au matin raie ...*
>
> *Resplendent as the brightness*
> *Of the summer morning's sun ...*

As the splendor of the Virgin is made more glorious in contrast to the appearance of mortal men, and as the brightness of the morning sun seems more brilliant following the darkness of night, so the windows of Chartres appear more radiant as they are seen against an architectural setting designed to enhance their particular lights.

In this work we shall be concerned with the experience of seeing these windows. It is a very complicated experience, involving considerations beyond the glass itself. In particular we shall consider the source of light transforming this substance into a visible medium, the visual atmosphere of the cathedral, and, most complicated of all, our own optical responses. While excursions into the rich field of color symbolism and the metaphysics of light in the Middle Ages are tempting, we shall confine ourselves to visual phenomena, and even here many of our efforts will be exploratory and inconclusive.

At the outset we shall observe the atmosphere of interior light within the Cathedral, along with the general appearance of the windows as they affect our eyes. Problems of irradiation and glare will be considered, as well as general optical conditions affecting the visual reception of different colors and intensities. An honored theory about the visual and color properties of stained glass will then be examined and tested on the basis of phenomenological observations and by comparisons with researches in color by scientists of the nineteenth and twentieth centuries.

A close examination of Chartres glass will also be undertaken to observe surface conditions, color, and internal structure of selected fragments. Finally, the last section will deal with the choice and composition of colors in several representative panels, analyzing the use and arrangement of color as it is related to the meaning and expression of various scenes. A brief comparison will be made with the composition of color in stained glass after the twelfth century, especially in late medieval and Renaissance windows.

It is hoped that by this study of the early stained glass of Chartres our knowledge of its qualities and effects will tend to be more objective and revealing.

CHAPTER I

ON SEEING THE WINDOWS

THE stained glass of Chartres is generally regarded as superior to all other. It has been the subject of endless speculation concerning the causes—technical and artistic—for its unrivaled position and universal acclaim. While in no manner attempting to deny or minimize the importance of the translucent material (it will be considered in detail later), I wish to establish at the outset that the intrinsic nature of the glass of Chartres is only one reason for its great reputation. Glass of comparable quality may be found at Canterbury, Bourges, Angers, Sens, and Poitiers, among others, but at Chartres a distinctive and perhaps singular condition is obtained, for here, more than in any other church of the period, the glass is *visible*. I shall try to describe this particular condition of 'visibility' in the following pages.

A survey of the majority of English and French cathedrals shows a tragic history of destruction and replacement of windows, especially during the eighteenth century in France and the Cromwellian period in England, with the result that remaining examples of early glass are surrounded by later works which often detract from the true effect of these windows by interfering with their visibility. Chartres, on the other hand, is still in possession of most of its original fenestration and has the inestimable advantage of *ensemble*, an unbroken, unifying condition establishing a pervasive harmony in the interior and controlling the subdued atmosphere of light and color. In the great vessel of the Cathedral, no extraneous light is allowed to destroy this harmony.

Any person who has visited the Cathedral at the close of the First or Second World War will appreciate this. During the wars, of course, all the glass was removed and buried in mines or in the Cathedral's crypt, with a whitish, plastic screen called vitrex installed in its place. The resultant effect in the interior was forlorn, bleak, and inexpressively sad. Stripped of its adornment, the cathedral was strangely changed; the mystery and the wonder were no longer there.

7

Following the wars, the long and painstaking process of resetting the glass was begun. I spent several weeks at the Cathedral in 1947 when the work was in progress, climbing the scaffolds to observe and photograph the process of fixing the panels to the armatures, and observing the completed windows from various positions in the nave. At this time all of the aisle windows were in place, as well as those in the clerestory of the north side, and all the windows of the chancel. Still bare were the west windows, the *Rose of France* in the north transept, and several areas of the south clerestory.

With the ensemble still wanting, the glass could not speak. It was strangely muted, dull, and ineffectual, suffering from a condition which stained glass artists call 'surface light,' a distracting light from adjacent and lightly glazed areas shining upon the *interior* surfaces of completed windows, dissipating their color and altering their luminosity. Not until all of the windows were in place was this distraction eliminated, and once again the incomparable splendor of Chartres was able to shine forth.

This was a vivid demonstration of one of the principal factors contributing to the singular beauty of this interior, as well as a commentary on some of the reasons for the disappointing effect of other churches. Totally white or unglazed windows are not the only offenders: if a deeply colored lancet is in the presence of windows of lighter tonality—especially those with grays and yellows predominating—it will suffer and lose its essential character. The effect of the Sainte Chapelle in Paris is an illustration, for the colors of the windows in the upper church are dampened by lighter rays from the fifteenth-century rose window on the west wall. True, the surrounding buildings cast shade on the little chapel, and much of the 'thirteenth-century' glass is nineteenth, but if the luminosity of the intruding rose were subdued, it would bring about a transformation, causing one to think that these windows were of better quality. This circumstance occurs in the vast majority of churches, and especially in museums, where stained glass is cruelly treated by bathing it in surface light and, worst of all, by backing it frequently with artificial illumination.

Even at Chartres (fortunately in limited areas which do not

affect the main body of the church), the action of surface light can be observed. Several chapels of the south ambulatory, especially the westernmost chapel containing *St. Martin's Window*, have suffered a loss of one or two original windows, which were replaced in later centuries by a light grisaille to illuminate the sculpture of the choir screen. The remaining thirteenth-century glass—some of it of extraordinary quality—is tragically weakened and unable to assert itself—or rather, unable to be seen. This distinction is very important. When the more powerful light from opposite or adjacent windows casts a reflection of higher luminosity upon the interior surface of an old window, the spectator's eye adapts to the brighter light, failing to perceive the deep colors of the old glass. Being essentially a translucent medium, stained glass, unlike mosaics, does not benefit from the luster of surface light which gives added visual interest to reflecting media. The surface gloss on mosaics does not form a deadening film over large areas, for the irregular setting of the tesserae causes the reflected light to be broken up into twinkling and glittering effects which change with the movement of the spectator, enhancing and animating the scene before him and dematerializing the wall. Moreover, the reflected light does not vitiate the colors of mosaics, for the source light causing the reflection is the same one—with the same intensity—that brings out the color in the body of the tesserae. On the other hand, caught between exterior and interior illumination of vastly differing intensities, stained glass must favor the transmitted light in order to be seen. Interior surface gloss, in addition to reducing color values, has the unfortunate effect of reminding the spectator of flat vitreous enclosures, denying the aesthetic of an art intended to create an ambience of wondrous and celestial light, unbounded, interpenetrating and transcending all things.

Another hazard in the seeing of windows is the phenomenon called glare. Imagine, for example, a church with all of its windows installed, and all of them belonging to the same category of colors and intensities. No surface light or other visual imbalance is allowed to disrupt the interior except in the case of one window which, we shall say, has suffered damage. Perhaps a small panel has been removed temporarily to repair the leading or to replace a missing fragment. When one looks at this window—even if the blank spot is only a fraction of the total area—it will be impossible to see its true colors. If the sun is shining on the window, the effect will be disastrous. Here it is important to recognize that with or without the blank area the colors in the separate pieces of glass actually remain the same: the same intensities, values, and hues are still there, with the same amount of light passing through them—this can be established by any measuring device. But, to the observer, they *are* changed—at times quite radically—and this brings us to the heart of the matter, for these colors and lights are not autonomous elements acting independently upon each other (as we speak of colors 'asserting themselves,' or going dull, or of the blue dominating the red, and so on), but for our purposes it is important to remember that these apparent changes *occur in the eye*, which has such unusual powers of adjustment that we are sometimes unaware of the rapid changes taking place.

At Chartres our eyes are called upon to make enormous adjustments, both in the quantitative and the qualitative sense. Let us speak for a moment about the quantitative measurement of light, with its accompanying demands upon our vision. Physicists tell us that the brightness of sunlight in summer, around midday, ranges from 8,000 to 10,000 foot-candles (horizontal meter reading) for temperate zones. I have taken meter readings outside the Cathedral on bright days during May and June, with intensities registering from 8,000 to 9,000 foot-candles. In contrast to this, in the dimly lighted nave of the Cathedral, the amount of light, according to my meter, has averaged between one and two foot-candles, occasionally less. Rarely is it above five foot-candles. In darker areas of the aisles, especially in the north ambulatory, my meter (which begins at one foot-candle) will not register anything. Anyone who has attempted to take photographs in the interior of this Cathedral will, I believe, verify my observations. There are times when one cannot even see the dial on the meter, or any of the figures printed on it.

This muted atmosphere creates enormous tasks for the eye. When the spectator enters the Cathedral from the bright sunlight, his vision must adjust rapidly to an illumination level several thousand times less than average daylight intensities. Immediately, he is struck by the richness and vibrancy of the windows, surrounded, however, by architectural features which cannot be made out too clearly. The interior is dim and vague, and the visitor must step with caution until his eyes have made a partial dark adaptation—which will take a few minutes, and as much as fifteen minutes in some cases—and then the details of the interior will seem clearer and lighter, while at the same time the windows become richer and more intense. The flexibility of the eye has made it possible to span this vast range of intensities with apparently little effort, so subtly achieved, indeed, that many spectators are unaware of it.

More rapid still is the adaptation of the eye when one returns to the outside. Here the adjustment is very quick and noticeable—sometimes causing momentary discomfiture or actual pain—for within one minute the average eye makes the transition from one or two foot-candles to eight or ten thousand, depending on the position and intensity of the sun, after which the eye is able to function efficiently. This common, yet extraordinary adjustment is accomplished with dispatch, serving as another illustration of the unusual powers of the human eye.

While the eye is capable of rapid sequential adjustment to widely varying intensities of light, it does, nevertheless, have a limitation of vital significance to anyone who would understand the basic problems of seeing stained glass. The eye can move from bright to dark and back again with remarkable efficiency, but it cannot be exposed to widely varying intensities in the same field *at the same time* without considerable loss in acuity and color perception. Therefore, in the case of a church with light windows surrounding a darker one, or in the instance of a richly colored window with an intruding spot of light glass, the eye will adapt to the brightest intensity of a given field or area, thus failing to perceive the more muted and perhaps richer tones in the same field. It takes only one offending bright area to spoil the effect of an entire ensemble if the rays passing through that area can reach the eye of the observer. A satisfactory analogy may be borrowed from music—from an instrument in the Cathedral itself, the pipe organ. If the organist is playing softly on the *dulciana*, and suddenly a cypher develops in a *diapason*, the single blast from this powerful pipe will overwhelm the softer tones so that they will scarcely be heard, if at all, though they continue to be sounded as before. The ear has adapted to the stronger sound as the eye adapts to the brighter light, and in both instances the intended effect has been shattered.

The superior visibility of the windows of Chartres is due in large measure to the absence of intruding surface light and glare. While rarely applicable to the other arts, the phenomenon of glare is a hazard frequently encountered in stained glass. The action of surface light is sometimes mentioned in the literature of this art, but the equally important factor of glare is not given equal emphasis—an unfortunate omission, for herein lies one explanation for the effectiveness or the failure of many windows.[1]

Glare is caused by a disproportionate mixture of high and low luminosities in the same visual field which go beyond the normal adaptive powers of the eye. Scientific literature is helpful in this area: glare is described as resulting from 'extreme variations in intensity occurring in the field of vision which produce disturbing effects upon the eye . . . contributing to ocular inefficiency and the production of fatigue. This is especially true where the eye in its movements must subject the central portion of the retina to frequent and sudden changes in stimulus intensities; its inability to meet these demands for rapid adjustment results in a temporary partial blindness—a central scotoma. Glare and its evil consequences are the result of useless illumination in the field of vision.'[2] Bontemps, the nineteenth-century chemist and authority on glass, had already applied these observations to stained glass: '. . . [moreover,] an artist attempting to achieve harmony through violent contrasts of bright and dark colors, and using uncontrolled light, will produce a panel fatiguing to the eye, causing the spectator to long for the serenity of older windows.'[3]

Central to this problem is the fact that stained glass is illuminated by light sources normally too intense for the eye to tolerate in direct perception (daylight illumination varies from 1,000 foot-candles on cloudy days to 10,000 foot-candles in bright sunlight), but illuminating engineers and physicians tell us that brightnesses ranging from thirty to seventy foot-candles are recommended for normal tasks of the human eye, such as reading, sewing, and the like. This is also the desired illumination in art galleries (actually, many are lower than this) in which paintings are seen by *reflected* light, another vastly significant distinction between the two arts. Therefore, the art of stained glass is confronted by optical problems rarely encountered in other arts, with glare being one of the most common hazards.

To illustrate this distinction, let us imagine a panel painting on display in a gallery illuminated at about forty foot-candles. Because of the absorption factor in reflected light, the brightest areas in the painting—even those appearing pure white—will reflect no more than fifty percent of the light, while most of the colors will absorb at least ninety percent of the incident light, with less than ten percent reflected. Therefore, with a brightness range of approximately twenty to four foot-candles (a ratio of five to one), the powers of the eye in this particular situation are in no way strained.

However, if the same subject were transposed to the medium of stained glass, the problems would be multiplied. Assume that the panel is set against a hazy sun of 4,000 foot-candle brightness. If clear glass is used in or near the visible field, it will transmit from eighty to ninety percent of the light. Opalescent glass, depending on the type, will transmit from fifty-five to eighty-five percent, while deep blues and reds will transmit from five to ten percent or less.[4] These are measurements made close to the transmitting surfaces, but at a distance the difference is intensified because of the irradiation of the brightest lights, already too strong for comfortable accommodation by the eye. Adaptation to high intensities is further complicated by the fact that the observer is located in an atmosphere of low luminosity (the interiors of most churches are twenty foot-candles, or much less), thus a jump to several thousand foot-candles is impossible without discomfort and a serious loss of perception in the lower levels where the deeper colors are registered.

Rarely does a work of art create the optical condition in which it is seen, but this is common with stained glass. While in a gallery there are, of course, many subtle visual interactions between adjacent paintings, colors of walls and floors, hangings, and so on—with all these elements contributing to the total effect—the light source in a gallery is normally separate and relatively colorless, coming from daylight, or from artificial or mixed sources, and falling upon the object without impinging upon the eye of the spectator. The spectator thus receives his impressions of the work of art through reflected light. The intensity of illumination, moreover, is ordinarily at a 'normal' and efficient level, often consistently maintained, thus causing little or no strain upon our adaptive optical mechanism.

A well-glazed cathedral, on the other hand, with its dimly lighted interior, causes within the eye a series of profound physical and physiological alterations, and among these is a lower adaptation level which makes the retina even more sensitive to intruding glare spots.[5] In ordinary experience—to draw an analogy from everyday life—every motorist knows that automobile headlights can be tolerated very easily in daytime, but at night, when the eye is dark-adapted, the effect of the same headlights is blinding. In experiments with white light and colored lights, Professor Hartridge shows an inverse ratio between the increase of white light and the perception of colored lights, with the blues especially weakened as the white light increases.[6]

Glare, therefore, attacks the viewer of stained glass when he is least able to bear it. It is also for this reason that a stained glass artist should consider, over and above the design of a particular window, the light milieu of an entire structure, and especially the conditions of light in the specific area where the window will be installed. Careless juxtaposition will be disastrous, both from the aesthetic and optical viewpoint. This is one reason that the mixture of medieval and Renaissance windows is seldom successful, for one destroys the effect of the other. (Parenthetically, I would like to state that I do not agree with many writers who look upon Renaissance windows as 'decadent,' for they are perfectly in accord with certain religious and aesthetic requirements of their time.) Often, however, they are ill-served by poor installation or unfortunate juxtaposition. Admittedly, late Gothic or Renaissance windows with lighter

values and greater tendencies toward naturalism—especially
in landscape scenes—present more pitfalls for glare, but the
effect can be very pleasant if the entire luminosity of the
window is kept at a tolerable level, without too wide a
range, and if it is shown in a well-lighted interior. Once
again it is the ensemble that matters. In many instances
a window is not decadent, but simply difficult to look at.
From a technical standpoint, it is normally desirable to adjust
brightness variations to the accommodation range of the eye,
but this does not mean that a window and its setting must
necessarily be low-keyed. The entire level of all the elements
may be raised, and the eye will operate within that range, as
in some of the delightful rococo interiors of the eighteenth
century, with golds and pastels on windows and walls, brightness and lightness everywhere. On the other hand, the Baroque
period, with its love of dramatic contrast—in sound, in mass, in
movement—also used light in a startling manner, employing
normally undesirable contrasts of brightness to great advantage, producing halation and irradiation effects especially in
window areas above main altars. The most famous instance is
the *Gloria* in St. Peter's in Rome, an oval window in light gold
above the Chair of St. Peter which, in brilliant sunlight, over-
flows its borders and spills out with awesome power over the
surrounding sculpture of gilt and bronze. Here, light becomes
an almost physical force with an overpowering visual impact,
serving as a dramatic, unifying element in the exuberant and
dynamic spirit of the Baroque. Gothic windows of the twelfth
and thirteenth centuries, however, call for an entirely different
treatment.

In the nave of Chartres, no extraneous light is allowed to
break the spell. The heavily saturated reds and blues glow
uninterruptedly in a low-keyed atmosphere created by deep,
translucent colors infinitely varied in hue, yet carefully ordered
within a harmonious scale of intensities. A mood is established
by shielding out all natural light, thereby transforming the vast
interior into a mysterious region of shadowy form and glowing
color. The eye perceives no surface illumination defining boundaries or revealing the physical function of glazed enclosures;
rather, one receives an impression of softly diffused, unbounded

luminosity 'pervading the interior beauty,' transforming and uniting all things.

Thus far we have been looking at the windows in terms of quantitative light: the amount of luminosity in the architectural interior, intensities from adjacent and opposite windows, glare spots, and so forth. In this experience the eye has demonstrated superior powers of adaptation, moving over a wide range of intensities with remarkable efficiency and little apparent effort. More wondrous still, and infinitely more subtle, are the qualitative modulations occurring in our eyes as we adjust to successive changes in brightness—especially from light to dark— for herein is a partial explanation for the mood we experience upon entering an interior like the nave of Chartres.

In order to appreciate the nature of these optical modifications, let us turn for a moment to pertinent observations by scientists. Von Helmholtz, in carefully controlled experiments, has found that the human eye increases in sensitivity to light at a rapid and phenomenal rate when the subject is placed in darkness.[7] Within four minutes the sensitivity increases seventy-five times, in fourteen minutes to 10,400, and at the end of thirty-one minutes it is 174,000 times greater. In another experiment, in which a group of subjects had been adapted to a dark room for one hour, the sensitivity to light was 'increased anywhere from fifty to 150,000 times.' Along with this quantitative change, a qualitative alteration takes place in the eye directly related to our subject.

Focillon describes the effect created by early stained glass windows as 'un crépuscule multicolore.'[8] Grodecki echoes similar observations, with specific reference to Chartres, comparing the interior brightness of the Cathedral during the war to its normal appearance: '... cette cathédrale était d'une clarté intérieure éblouissante; regarnie de vitraux, elle a repris son atmosphère incertaine, entre le jour et le crépuscule.'[9]

'An uncertain atmosphere, between day and twilight.' Grodecki has observed an effect of light and color in the Cathedral which has interested scientists for many years, called in popular language 'twilight vision.' 'Twilight vision' is a moderate form of retinal change known as the Purkinje phenomenon or Purkinje shift, from the researches of the Czech scientist, Jan Evangelist Purkinje, who, early in the nineteenth century, was the first to make a concentrated study of the qualitative effects of dark adaptation[10]—although observers as far back as Aristotle had recorded certain phenomenological observations of color changes under subdued light, especially at twilight.[11]

The Purkinje phenomenon occurs most vividly in extreme states of light and dark adaptation, called by scientists photopic and scotopic vision. Briefly stated—without going into the vastly complicated problems of rod and cone function, peripheral and foveal vision, etc.—the human eye tends to perceive the central colors of the spectrum (the green-yellow area) as brighter during photopic vision, but under dark-adapted or scotopic vision a 'shift' occurs in the luminosity curve towards the blue-violet end of the spectrum, with these colors appearing to be brighter. A simple demonstration of this shift can be made with two pieces of colored cloth, approximately similar in value and saturation but differing in hue. I have made it with small pieces of cloth of the same manufacture, one red and one blue (representing opposite ends of the spectrum), which appear equally bright under daylight illumination, but on awakening at night—when my eyes are totally dark-adapted after several hours of sleep—and looking at these cloths in the dark they seem colorless; but the blue cloth is much brighter on the gray scale than the red, which appears very dark, almost black. In dim light the colors begin to assert themselves, but at low luminosities the blue still seems brighter. Furthermore, under dark-adaptation, there is a general vagueness in the perception of form, and outlines cannot be seen too distinctly, a condition attributed by scientists to the dominance of peripheral vision, which is not as high in acuity as the central area of the retina which mediates daytime vision.

This can be applied to stained glass. While I have never slept in a cathedral (it has been done!), I did have the good fortune several summers ago to stay in an old house which had a stained glass window in the living room, and during several sleepless nights I spent considerable time observing this window in absolute darkness—or rather, in nighttime darkness, which is somewhat lighter. The same phenomenon observed with the cloths occurred: the blue family of colors were seen as bright patches of gray wherever they appeared in the window. The middle colors of the spectrum remained moderately light, but those toward the red end were dark, with heavily saturated reds appearing almost black, seemingly opaque. The leading was also indistinct, fuzzy and blurred in outline.

These experiences are useful in describing certain reactions to more or less absolute states of light and dark adaptation, but we must now attempt to apply these observations to more normal conditions in viewing stained glass; namely, with daylight coming through the windows. In the case of a church with high luminosity in the nave and bright windows as well, there is no complication, for the eyes are operating consistently on a photopic level, but in the dimly lighted interior of Chartres our eyes make a partial scotopic adaptation which has a pervasive effect on our sense impressions while we are there. A phenomenon occurs involving the two visual states, for, as scientists tell us, there are many degrees in dark and light adaptation involving both the photopic and scotopic systems, and both states can be in existence simultaneously. Some refer to this condition in which the two systems participate, as the mesopic intensity level.[12]

Most people, on entering the Cathedral, are struck by the overwhelming color of the stained glass as it is set off brilliantly against the darkness of the interior—a vast space filled with shadowy and indistinct forms punctuated at rhythmic intervals by these incomparable windows. Has color ever been presented with such *éclat*? Where can one find such brilliance, and so much of it, in such a setting? It is not surprising that many visitors have burst into tears upon experiencing this sight for the first time, as I have witnessed on more than one occasion.

After the first impression, the visitor proceeds to walk slowly through the interior—down the nave or across the transept, in the aisles or around the ambulatory, pausing here and there, and then going on. At first he proceeds rather cautiously, especially if he is near the steps joining the aisles to the nave at the west end, for he will not be able to see these steps distinctly, and will negotiate them gingerly. After the visitor has remained inside the Cathedral for fifteen minutes or more—a half an hour is better, an hour still better—his eyes will begin to distinguish architectural and sculptural details not too clearly seen when he first entered. The proportioning of the nave, the elevations, the ribbed vaults, and massive supporting piers are more distinct, and the structural clarity of the building has begun to assert itself. The visitor can also see more of the texture and surfacing of wall areas, as well as something of the stone floor of the Cathedral. However, none of these are seen with absolute clarity, for all of the architectural components are bathed in a rich reddish-blue or bluish-red light from the windows (at times, purplish in effect) not in the form of direct rays of color (old glass does not do this) but in a kind of diffused, pervasive glow of warm color ... low-keyed, somewhat intangible and illusive in character.

A partial dark-adaptation has taken place, with a lowered threshold of vision, allowing the spectator to see more of his surroundings, and a kind of revelatory process, in the optical sense, has occurred. All the while he has been able to see the windows as well as before—or so it seems. Actually a subtle change has occurred here, too, but we are much less aware of it, for our color memories do not serve us as well as our recollections of tangible things. The steps, walls, and piers are there for constant reference (for verification by touch, if necessary), but our impressions of color and light are evanescent, changing ever so subtly, and difficult to record with exactitude as they modulate before our eyes. Even if we were to stand in front of the same window and make color notes over a period of thirty minutes we would have in the end a series of word descriptions which would not be as vivid as the actual visual experience, and it would be difficult to reconstruct in one's memory the original color impressions received, however accurate we tried to be. Our color memories can be very deceptive, especially when describing a series of color changes in combination over a period of time. How, then, can we attempt to approximate our changing impressions of a window from the time we first saw it with our light-adapted eyes to a later moment when our eyes are partially dark-adapted? What has happened in the way we see it?

This is possible, to a certain extent, by means of a rather picturesque experiment. Our eyes, fortunately, can in some ways operate independently: for example, one eye can be dark-adapted while at the same time the other eye operates on a photopic level. By wearing an eye patch over one eye for at least fifteen minutes before entering a cathedral, it will be possible to look at the windows first with your light-adapted eye, and then with your dark-adapted one. When this is done in quick alternation it produces some curious impressions.

In order to appreciate the difference between a normal and dark-adapted eye in the perception of this interior, I have dark-adapted one eye for fifteen minutes before arriving at the Cathedral by bandaging it, thereby closing it and shielding it from all light. Upon entering the Cathedral from the bright outdoors, I immediately looked at one of the north clerestory windows with my light-adapted eye, observing the details and the colors. Then I removed the bandage from my other eye, and looked at the same window. The difference was startling. First of all, I was surprised by the comparative lightness of the surrounding architecture, which to the other eye was nothing but a dark enclosure for the windows. Next, I was struck by the alteration of the colors, for the blues seemed to establish the tone of the whole window, while before there seemed to be a more even balance between the reds and the blues. The reds were definitely tinged with violet, in contrast to the pure reds previously seen by my light-adapted eye. Moreover, there was a blurring of edges and lines, something of an overlapping of colors (especially during the first few seconds of exposure of the dark-adapted eye when it was probably getting into focus) but the blurring persisted for a short time thereafter. The entire effect differentiating one eye from the other would disappear within thirty seconds if the second eye were exposed for that length of time without interruption, but more time for observations was gained by exposing it for only a few seconds each time and then shielding it again, thereby allowing time for alternate observations by both eyes.

While the above experiment affords the most dramatic contrasts by comparing in rapid succession the impressions of separately exposed eyes in extreme states, it is not realistic for the particular light characteristics of a given interior. There-fore, I then adapted both eyes to the interior light of the Cathedral for at least half an hour, after which I closed and shielded one eye—in order to keep it adapted to the interior light—then went outside and adapted the other eye to the external light for at least one minute, and returned to the Cathedral's nave. First I observed with the light-adapted eye, then with the other. In this case, the difference was not so extreme. There was a slight blurring of lines, especially in the black outlines of the leads, and the architectural surroundings were again a fraction lighter, but no radical color shift was observed between the two eyes. Some of the reds, especially in the smaller areas, shifted slightly toward the blue, but in general they retained their strength and richness, while the blues gained slightly in luminosity. Only in acuity was there a noticeable change, and this was not as pronounced as in the first experiment. Undoubtedly, if other observers were to par-ticipate in experiments of this type, many variations from my own impressions would be reported (especially with respect to the color shift) attesting to a wide variation in individual reaction.

Studies of vision in the intermediate or mesopic range be-tween absolute light and dark adaptation seem to point to a heightened receptivity in the red and yellow-green areas of the spectrum, while at the same time the eye retains much of its scotopic sensitivity to the blue wavelengths.[13] Therefore in this condition—which I believe is the optical situation inside the Cathedral of Chartres—the eye experiences in successive stages a heightened sensitivity to all colours, with maximum recep-tivity after about half an hour inside the Cathedral.

Our discussion has not taken into account the phenomena of after-images, fatigue, color deterioration, and so forth, all form-ing part of our visual experience in viewing stained glass. But for the purposes of this study we have placed more emphasis on general observations concerning the ensemble of light and color, surface light, glare, visual adaptation, and qualitative alteration in color under certain conditions. Therefore, a few additional observations may be pertinent.

We have seen that the semi-darkness within the Cathedral

C

contributes frequently to changing modes of color perception, accompanied by an appreciable drop in visual acuity. Directly related to the latter condition are observations made by Wald and Griffin on the subject of visual acuity in dim light, in which they state that under these conditions the eye is in a state of relative myopia: 'In dim light the eye enters a state of relatively fixed focus, little different from its condition when the accommodation is paralyzed with homatropine.'[14] The authors attribute this less to the dilation of the pupil than to increased aberration within the refractive system of the eye. These observations were based on *amounts* of light, in this case a small amount of light affecting optical responses in a certain manner.

Also pertinent are experiments in visual acuity involving qualitative distinctions: specifically, a series of observations of the human eye and its responses under various colored lights. 'It may be stated as a general principle that the retina shows greater instability in retaining its resolving power under colored light than under white light, and that this instability is greater for some colors than for others.'[15] In one experiment the following colors were used: red, orange, yellow, yellow-green, green, blue-green, and blue, at two intensities of light—0.81 and 3.35 meter-candles. It was found that yellow was highest in acuity rating, followed by yellow-green, orange, and green, in that order. Lowest were the deep reds, the blue-greens, and the blues, the latter being the lowest of all. Therefore, we find that the colors affording the least acuity to the eye are the hues dominating the color ensemble of Chartres: blue and red—with their resultant and complicating mixtures—all adding to the confusion of our senses and the blurring of our perceptions during our stay in this interior. Consonant with these observations are comments by Professor David Katz on seeing the surfaces of metallic objects in dim and colored lights, a mode of appearance which he calls a 'weird luminosity,' an intangible glow which ordinarily is luster in a bright light, but which in subdued illumination is transformed to a more mysterious luminosity.[16]

Recalling my own experiences in studying the glass of Chartres Cathedral, I remember that my eyes would become fatigued if I tried to make out details in the windows for any length of time. The opaque painting of draperies and features, and the leads themselves, seemed more distinct at the start of my examinations—when I had come in from the outside—than toward the end. Undoubtedly, in adapting to the darkened interior and in simultaneously perceiving the whole range of the spectrum in transmitted light, my eyes were confronted with a formidable task. During my hours on the scaffolds photographing the west windows, when my narrow platform was illuminated solely by the diffused and heavily saturated colors, I was sometimes affected by a mild sense of vertigo; for in addition to the elevation, the visual atmosphere was uncertain, especially during periods of very high or very low illumination. I remember a blurring of vision, a loss of acuity after long exposure to the glass either at close or at long range.

The widely varying intensity levels and color tonalities of different interiors undoubtedly affect the quality of our visual responses to all objects in view. In contrast to our experience at Chartres, we encounter a different atmosphere in an interior illuminated by lighter windows favoring the middle range of the spectrum—the yellows, golds and greens—in which all things are seen with greater clarity and exactitude, an optical condition appropriate to structures belonging to periods other than the one we have considered. The Renaissance, for example, used lighter windows for more clearly illuminated interiors, enhancing three-dimensional form and revealing the classic order, the carefully adjusted proportions, and the clarity of the building's scale. If man was to be in the center of the world, he wanted to be seen there, in the midst of his works. As in the frescoes of Masaccio, where figures take on more tangible form and even cast shadows through the artist's rendition of natural light, so in architectural interiors the admittance of greater amounts of daylight is consonant with the rational order of the building and its manifest concern with human scale. It is also the appropriate illumination for the viewing of three-dimensional sculpture displayed throughout the building.

Conversely, Renaissance sculpture shown in dim Gothic interiors suffers enormously, for its plastic form cannot assert itself without the aid of a definable light source with its resultant highlights and shadows. It is as if the actors in a drama appeared on an unlighted stage. This is demonstrated at Chartres by the sixteenth-century sculpture on the choir screen around the ambulatory, excellent examples of the *détente* style that suffer in a light milieu out of key with the aesthetic intention. This visual incompatibility, along with unfavorable comparisons with the distinguished Gothic sculpture of the Cathedral, has placed this later work in disgrace.

Old stained glass, because of the density and irregularity of the material, holds back or disperses most of the light acting upon it, resulting not only in low luminosities but in a vagueness of form for all objects perceived. Without strong and consistent light source, the elements of the interior are not seen in consistent and predictable patterns of highlights and shadows that define forms and enhance their three-dimensionality. Rather, perceived outlines become blurred and shadowy. This unusual light also affects the visitor who himself undergoes a kind of metamorphosis, for he does not cast a definable shadow in this mysterious and diffused glow, the optical laws governing daylight having been rearranged and held back. As in the manuscript illumination and sculpture of the early Gothic period, we witness a transformation of appearance, a reordering of things as we know them.

It was in such a setting that Abbot Suger of Saint-Denis experienced his *ascensio*, as related in his *Book of Administration*: 'Thus when—out of my delight in the beauty of the house of God—the loveliness of the many-coloured gems has called me away from external cares, and worthy meditation has induced me to reflect, transferring that which is material to that which is immaterial, on the diversity of sacred virtues; then it seems to me that I see myself dwelling, as it were, in some strange region of the universe which neither exists entirely in the slime of the earth nor entirely in the purity of Heaven; and that, by the grace of God, I can be transported from this inferior to that higher world in an anagogical manner.'[17]

Many visitors to Chartres have experienced in various ways something of the exaltation described in the Neoplatonic language of Abbot Suger. The subdued interior, with its heavily saturated colors, provides a setting conducive to the mystical experience, with all earthly light transformed and all objects vaguely perceived, producing in the observer a kind of visual intoxication. Little wonder that descriptions of psychological and emotional states are commonly expressed in various metaphors of light and color. Moreover, heavily saturated reds and blues, as they are used here, seem to be more emotionally charged than lighter colors, and play effectively upon our senses.

So impressive are these windows that many interpretations and theories have arisen to account for their extraordinary beauty—especially ideas concerning the intrinsic superiority of the glass, the possible use of precious stones in the glass itself, and the application of certain formulas of light and color in the composition of these panels. Some writers have advanced hypothetical rules and laws to account for the excellence of these windows, and by far the most influential writer in this category was the nineteenth-century French authority, Eugène Emmanuel Viollet-le-Duc, whose article *Vitrail* has gained widespread acceptance in Europe and America. I shall devote the next chapter to an examination of these theories.

CHAPTER II

THE STAINED GLASS THEORIES OF
VIOLLET-LE-DUC

In his youth, Viollet-le-Duc spent long periods at Chartres, sketching the architecture and sculpture of the Cathedral and observing the famous windows. A letter to his father, written in his twenty-first year, is full of enthusiasm as he records his impressions of the Cathedral and its art: '... *tout cela me fait vibrer le cœur et me plonge dans des pensées d'une douceur inexprimable.*'[1] Similar passages of poetic feeling occur in other letters from this period, episodes of subjective reflection which may surprise admirers of the man who later became the leading exponent of rationalism in architecture. In those days, according to one of his biographers, he was '*subjugué par sa sensibilité d'artiste, mais rien dans ses appréciations ne fait encore présager sa découverte de la méthode de composition qui distingue cette œuvre admirable des productions architecturales du genre classique.*'[2]

Soon, however, these youthful subjugations were to pass away. Two of his succeeding years were spent in Rome, where already the mature man began to emerge. While his fellow students at the Villa Medici were copying Raphael in the *Loggie* and *Stanze* of the Vatican, Viollet-le-Duc busied himself with more practical matters in a thorough survey of '*le système d'égouts employé par les Romains.*'[3] In spite of his exposure to the ancient glories of Rome and his friendship with ardent classicists like Ingres, Viollet-le-Duc returned to France in the fall of 1837 to begin his extensive studies of Gothic architecture, comparing it favorably with the Classic in a manner recalling a kindred spirit in England, A. W. N. Pugin, who had published his *Contrasts* not long before.

The 1840's witnessed his activities as an official and later as head of the restoration program for the *Commission des Monuments Historiques*, which included many of the best known monuments of medieval France. Chartres and its windows were given special attention during the years 1842–1845, a period when restorations at Amiens, Sens, Toulouse, and Carcassonne were also accomplished. Fortunately in comparatively good state of preservation, Chartres did not receive the drastic attentions visited upon many of these monuments, especially Carcassonne and Pierrefonds, which today impress us as costly examples of nineteenth-century fantasy. Unlike Saint-Denis, the twelfth- and thirteenth-century windows of Chartres were still in place, needing only patchwork for fractured and missing pieces of glass, as well as the strengthening and replacement of supporting armatures and the restoration of certain areas of border decoration. On the whole this work was conscientious, with the obvious attempts to imitate the colors and painting styles of the medieval glassmaker achieved with varying degrees of success. A close examination of the panels will allow one to detect quite easily the restored painting in heads, draperies, and decorative details, but fortunately these additions do not detract from the total impression of the windows when viewed in ensemble from a normal position in the Cathedral. Some of the border restorations are excellent, and the newer glass is fortunately unassertive, generally absorbed into the totality of color.

During this period as *Inspecteur Général of the Commission des Monuments Historiques,* Viollet-le-Duc conceived the idea of his dictionary, the famous and vastly influential *Dictionnaire raisonné de l'architecture française,*[4] a nine-volume work which was to dominate architectural thinking (in particular the interpretation of Gothic architecture) for almost a century. The writing began in 1848, and the separate volumes were published between 1854 and 1868. Volume nine, dated 1868, contains the article, *Vitrail,* an exposition of basic laws and principles which, according to Viollet-le-Duc, account for the superiority of medieval stained glass. On the basis of examples chosen for illustrations, and because of certain phenomenological observations recorded in the text, it is apparent that Chartres was the principal source for this article—the twelfth-century glass in particular—for no other cathedral has a comparable ensemble from this period.

Recalling his work on Gothic architecture, the stained glass theories of Viollet-le-Duc have dominated subsequent study of this subject. In *Vitrail* one encounters the same apparent logic and thoroughgoing system found in the more famous section under *Construction*, written in a similarly powerful and convincing style. Frequently he has been cited as the greatest and final authority on both, and only during the second quarter of the twentieth century have his views on architecture been widely challenged. His theories concerning stained glass have continued to enjoy an unquestioned acceptance from the majority of historians and artists in the field. The leading European authority, Louis Grodecki, states that 'The admirable article *Vitrail* should be cited above all modern studies,'[5] and in the introduction to the catalogue of the *Vitraux de France* exhibition in 1953, Grodecki writes: 'The problem of unequal luminosity of colors was of great concern to the stained glass artists of the Middle Ages; Viollet-le-Duc has made an admirable analysis of the technical demands of this art...'[6] Jean Verrier speaks of Theophilus and Viollet-le-Duc in the same sentence, referring to the article of the latter as 'of capital importance for the comprehension of the irradiation of colors upon each other...'[7] Marcel Aubert echoes similar ideas.[8]

In America, the leading advocate of Viollet-le-Duc's theories was the late Charles Connick, who enlarged upon and illustrated these principles in a popular book.[9] More recently, another practicing artist in this medium, Robert Sowers, asserts that '*Vitrail* is still the most thorough and painstaking analysis of the medium of stained glass that has ever been written.'[10] General texts in art history, if they mention the art of stained glass at all, are usually under the spell of the great nineteenth-century Frenchman.

Viollet-le-Duc's *Vitrail* does not attempt a thorough chronological survey. Rather, it sets out to establish 'true principles' and laws for the successful practice of this art, using French windows from the twelfth and thirteenth centuries, especially the west windows of Chartres, as examples *par excellence* of a thoroughgoing application of these laws, resulting in a superior art contrasting brilliantly with 'decadent' works from the post-medieval period, apparently created by artists who had forgotten or abandoned these principles.

At the heart of his theory is the phenomenon of unequal

radiation of translucent colors. Viollet-le-Duc uses the word
rayonnant, but it is better translated into English in the sense of
irradiation, for he is referring to the apparent tendency of certain colors to spread out and encroach upon neighboring colors,
resulting in unexpected and at times unpleasant effects. 'Know-
ing therefore . . . the unequal powers of irradiation of colored
glass, the stained glass artists of the twelfth century created
their panels according to the way in which translucent colors
act upon each other.'[11] Blue is the color with the most powerful
qualities of irradiation and is therefore the color to be mastered
by the artist. Especially in juxtaposition with red—a color with
'feeble powers of irradiation'—the blue presents many problems, for if it is not properly controlled, the blue will spread
beyond its borders and overpower the reds and other adjacent
colours, according to this theory.

Concerning the apparent dominance of blue over other hues,
many visitors to the Cathedral of Chartres have noticed a
radical change in the color of the west windows when viewed
from a distance, especially from the crossing. When seen
nearby, from a point near the west wall, the colors—especially
the reds and blues—are deep, powerful and heavily saturated;
this is true also of the other colors, yellows, greens, purples . . .
all present in their strongest tones. But as one moves toward
the east end of the building, an alteration takes place, particularly with respect to the reds, which seem to grow darker as the
distance increases. Then, from the crossing, they are hardly to
be seen. From this viewpoint, the same windows have shifted
to another color category altogether, for they have lost their
individual values and now appear to be dominantly blue, but
not a deep, intense blue; rather, one sees a light and scintil-
lating effect in which all the colors have combined into a new
unity. Many observers, seeing these windows from the crossing,
refer to them as 'the blue windows'; others see them as a light
blue-green. No one, however, perceives any dominant coloration belonging to the red end of the spectrum. Is it possible that
this pronounced color change could have influenced Viollet-le-
Duc in his theories concerning the irradiating power of blue?

Viollet-le-Duc suggests the following experiments to illustrate his basic principles:

It is necessary to recognize that translucent colors have very different powers of irradiation. Thus, taking only the three fundamental colors of the spectrum—blue, yellow, and red—when these three colors are applied to glass and made translucent, they irradiate in different degrees. Blue is the color of greatest irradiation, red is very feeble, while yellow does not irradiate at all if it tends toward orange, and only a little if it is light yellow.

As an illustration, let us suppose that a stained glass panel is designed according to my Figure. The black lines indicate the strips of lead between the pieces of glass (see A). The areas R are red, those marked L blue, and the strips indicated by C white. In diagram B we see the effect produced by this panel when viewed at a distance of about sixty-five feet (twenty meters).

The circular areas of blue (L) irradiate to the circumference indicated by the dotted lines, and the red areas remain unaffected only in the middle of each piece (R). The result is as follows: all surfaces indicated by (O) are red overpowered by blue, producing a violet effect; the thin strips of white between the colors are lightly tinged with blue in the area (V), as well as the leads themselves, and the general effect of this panel will be cold and violet-tinged in most areas, with the red spots strident if you are near the window, somber if you are far away.

But if (see A) we decrease the area of the blue discs (L) with dark paint as in (D), we neutralize in part the irradiating effect of these blue disks. If in the place of the white strips (C) we place strips tinted with yellow or green, and if we trace on these strips thin lines as in (e), or pearling as in (f), then we obtain a much better effect. The blues, surrounded by these bold, opaque patterns and restrained by painted designs within the disks, are deprived of their irradiating power. The reds are much less influenced by their proximity. The yellowish- or greenish-whites of the strips are enhanced by the neighboring blues which sharpen their extremities, retaining between these extremities a warm area uniting these sections with the reds, especially if we have been careful to augment the value of the leads by the use of pearling or other simple patterns.

In contrast, let us suppose that the square areas (R) in plan A are blue, and the disks (L) red. Seen from a distance, the blues, with their power of irradiation, overcome the reds to such a degree that the latter appear black or dark violet, so that one would not suspect the presence of red in this panel. The white strips appear a dirty grey, or greenish if they are yellow tinted, or green-blue if they are tinged with green. The effect will be unpleasant, and without contrast. The irradiation of the blue weakens and spoils the other hues, which in turn are deprived of their power to enhance the purity and transparency of the blues. In general the color effect will be cold, gummy, with a false tonality; for, in stained glass, more than in panel painting, the value of each tone depends in large part on the opposition of another. A light blue near a greenish-yellow becomes turquoise; the same blue near a red becomes azure blue. A red near a light yellow seems to take on an orange cast, but turns violet when juxtaposed with blue.

These elementary principles, and others which we will soon develop, were practiced by the stained glass artists of the twelfth century, with a mastery that could come only from a long series of observations. We do not believe that they had a written theory, a kind of scientific treatise, as we have in our time. Rather, they worked according to an experimental method, and in this way developed traditions perpetuated in their ateliers.[12]

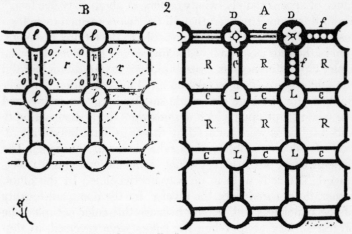

Diagram from Viollet-le-Duc, *Vitrail*, p. 379

In order to make an informal test of the experiment described in the above quotation, I commissioned a stained glass artist[13] to make up a panel according to the specifications of Viollet-le-Duc, following the design of his Figure. No exact size for the panel or its component sections was stipulated by Viollet-le-Duc, therefore it was decided to cut the glass in a manner proportionate to the average size of twelfth-century glass components in the west windows of Chartres, which I have had the opportunity to examine at close range on scaffolds. In our panel, the red squares were 4″ × 4″, and the blue circles 1⅞″ in diameter.[14] The measurement of the entire panel was 2′ × 1′ 7″. As for the colors, again there was no exact specification given in *Vitrail*, except 'red' and 'blue.' Using pieces of 'antique' glass—the modern glassworker's term for glass hand-blown in a manner intended to imitate medieval methods—we matched colors as closely as possible with fragments of

Chartres' twelfth-century reds and blues in my possession, and with these we made up the panel. (The Chartres fragments were too small to be used in this particular experiment.) The panel was installed in a window, against natural daylight, with the remaining area shielded by opaque material and curtains to eliminate distracting light from the surroundings.

According to directions, the panel was observed from a distance of approximately twenty meters, or about sixty-five feet.[15] From this point I noticed that all the colors seemed to suffer a loss in brightness, but I was not able to detect any discoloration in the reds as a result of the invasion of the blues. I saw no violet circumferences as a result of their juxtaposition, nor did the white strips seem to take on any blue coloration, however light. As for the blue disk made smaller by overpainting, and the white strips upon which designs were made, their visibility and brightness were reduced by this treatment, but no alteration of color was observed in other areas of the panel. The general effect of the glass did not seem cold, nor was it violet-tinged. The reds were in no way overwhelmed by the blues: rather, it appeared to be the reverse, for the dominant tonality of the panel was red, if only because this color occupied the largest surface area. When the colors were reversed, as described in the fifth paragraph of the *Vitrail* quotation (cited above), the dominant effect was blue, for the above reason, but I was not able to perceive any of the alterations and encroachments predicted in Viollet-le-Duc's text.

During the course of this experiment, and in order to check my own observations, I asked several friends to look at these panels. Of the ten or twelve individuals making these observations, not one was able to see any discoloration of the reds by the blues. However, several remarked that if there was any irradiation at all, it came from the white strips separating the main colors. Most of the witnesses reported a blurring of detail at that distance, and a loss of brightness, but none thought the total effect was unpleasant. Slight variations of opinion occurred in judging relative brightnesses between individual pieces of glass, pointing up normal differences in perception, but no one's reaction appeared to endorse the principles expressed in *Vitrail*.

While this experiment was admittedly inconclusive and un-scientific, lacking the proper controls and laboratory conditions, it nevertheless gave me some cause, through visual observation, to suspect the validity of this carefully constructed theory, so assuredly presented and so widely honored. It remained to test these theories against the windows themselves which served in large part as Viollet-le-Duc's models, and thus to determine the extent of their application. This was done on the basis of per-sonal observation in the Cathedral and through color photo-graphs taken of its stained glass at close range and at eye level on scaffolds erected for the purpose.

It is possible that the theories of Viollet-le-Duc have never been seriously challenged up to the present time for the reason that under normal conditions it has been impossible to make detailed observations of many of the windows he used as illus-trations. The twelfth-century examples at Chartres, with the exception of *La Belle Verrière*, are high above the heads of the spectators, the lowest panels being about thirty-five feet, and the uppermost panels almost seventy feet, from the floor of the nave, making a normal view possible only at a distance of a hundred feet or over. Until the time of Étienne Houvet, who was not able to make a complete record of the west windows, scholars had to use hand-painted reproductions in Durand's *Monographie*, published between 1867 and 1881, which were totally inadequate for a detailed and accurate study of the windows. Other handsome volumes of this period on French stained glass, like those of de Lasteyrie, Martin and Cahier, and Lévy, have beautiful plates which are a credit to the nineteenth-century artist-engraver but have little relationship to the color artistry of the medieval glass-worker. During the first half of the twentieth century, the most comprehensive work on Chartres glass was the Delaporte-Houvet publication, con-taining many photographs, largely black-and-white, with some rather inaccurate color plates. The study of his subject, there-fore, has been retarded by technical limitations which, on the other hand, have been no hindrance to the effective presenta-tion of the sculpture and architecture of the Cathedral.

Present-day color photography is a vast improvement in our equipment, but even the best work in this field falls short in capturing the subtle optical properties of stained glass. For example, printed color reproductions, however fine, are a negation of an art conceived primarily in terms of living, transmitted light, and not on the basis of reflected color printed on opaque surfaces. Color transparencies of excellent quality are more desirable, for with this medium the phenomenon of translucency is repeated, but even here there are limitations, for the dyes of color film can only approximate the dominant hues of each panel, rendering them in flat tones, without suggestion of the subtle modalities of color, the variations in saturation and luminosity, and above all the vibrancy so characteristic of this medium. The even, over-all emulsion of film restricts everything to its own tolerances, muting the brilliant spotting of flickering lights and colors and eliminating the suggestion of dichroism in old glass, rendering the whole in terms of flat and lifeless patterns. The best color transparency, for example, is not sufficiently sensitive to distinguish between old and new glass within a given area (except for pieces containing more recent painting of features, draperies, etc.), while in the presence of the actual glass panel, at close range, one can readily see the replacements without much difficulty. In spite of these limitations, however, we shall make use of certain color reproductions for some observations. Let us look at a few of these pictures.

Figure 1, the *Madonna and Child* panel from the central window, is part of the *Adoration of the Magi* series, flanked in the actual window by scenes depicting the arrival and departure of the Three Kings.

The robe of the Madonna is a deep magenta, and, in the original panel, that of the Child an ethereal blue—*bleu du ciel*. On either side of Mary the capitals surmounting the slender columns are a delicate violet, while the egg-and-dart banding under the clerestory motif to the left is a light blue. The blue ground of Chartres is deep and intense, but of an extraordinary vivacity brought about by spotted areas of brightness creating flickering patterns of light which are impossible for opaque reproductions to simulate. The blue in the color plate is much too light and flat. Moreover, the original panel, along with those that surround it, is suffused with light, weightless and without substance, its boundaries unstable and indeterminate as colors advance and recede and then seem suspended—the whole appearing to float in an unreal atmosphere in which normal spatial relationships cannot be established. In looking at the light-filled panel, one is not sure of the exact location of the inside surfaces of the colored glass: the heavily saturated rays issuing from them create something of a continuum between medium and milieu, confusing the spectator as to the beginning of one and the ending of the other. Seemingly advancing toward us is the golden throne of the Madonna, with its powerful yellows, and the deep tones of the Virgin's robe, along with her bright red halo and the red and golden sceptre, set against a blue ground which seems to recede into infinite space. Inconsistent with these general areas is a random spotting within them of different hues and values setting up opposing sub-motions unco-ordinated with the larger patterns, causing multiple oscillations in the visual field and compounding the physical instability of the scene. Consistent with this, the avoidance of normal perspective, the arbitrary proportioning of forms, and the shifting of the ground-line, make it impossible to establish a normative relationship between image and spectator. The elements advance and recede and move strangely about, not, of course, within the context of the physical word, but always in the realm of light.

All of this is lost to us, however, when we are forced to deal with opaque reproductions. Nevertheless, imperfect as they are, they do suggest general hue categories and are quite accurate in their representation of surface painting, hatching, and the location of leading and cross-bars. They will serve to a certain extent, therefore, in our examination of some of the theories on stained glass advanced by Viollet-le-Duc.

One of the basic premises of *Vitrail* is found in the following sentence: 'In fact, the juxtaposition of red and blue is perilous; it is a real dissonance, and it was with great ability that the stained glass artists of the twelfth and thirteenth centuries met this problem.'[16] Viollet-le-Duc goes on to say that the master glaziers of Chartres, Bourges, and other great French cathedrals, prevented the invasion of the reds by the blues through two principal devices: (1) the insertion of white strips or white beading between the two colors, as illustrated by the encircling band of red surrounded by white beading in Figure 1; and (2) the use of an overlay of hatching in the contiguous areas, especially on the blues, when the separating white strip is not present.

If we examine all of the panels in the central window of Chartres we will find that every one, round or square, uses white beaded enframements,[17] which would seem to support this theory. Whether the artists were concerned with the separation of colors or with a desire to establish twinkling effects of light in a window heavily saturated with deep color is a matter of opinion, and more about this will be said later. For the moment, let us examine the second device, concerning the hatching of contiguous areas. The magnificent *Annunciation* panel (Fig. 2) will serve as an example, for it is well preserved except for the nineteenth-century faces and some of the background red. In this scene there are large areas of juxtaposed red and blue: on both sides of the Angel Annunciate the solid red ground is close to his blue robe; this also applies to his halo, and to the blue cape worn by the Virgin. In none of these areas, neither in the red nor blue, is hatching used 'to prevent irradiation.' Nothing separates the colors except the usual leading, and the opaque painting appearing on the glass to render bodily parts and drapery folds is done according to Romanesque convention. Similarly, the elaborate garment of the Virgin in the *Presentation* scene (Fig. 3) seems to disregard this all-important principle. Many other examples could be cited, but these will suffice. Indeed, it is difficult to find anywhere in the original panels the use of hatching in the manner described by Viollet-le-Duc.

The French author does not attempt to account for the fact that this 'perilous' combination of reds and blues was, in practice, the favorite combination in French stained glass during the twelfth and thirteenth centuries, and is seen in all the great cathedrals still possessing their original windows. Red and blue, above all, dominate the supreme west windows of Chartres, and surely no unpleasant effects have been reported by centuries of admirers. Moreover, we may question whether a violet or reddish-purple tonality—if it did occur in any twelfth-century window—was necessarily regarded as undesirable, for in the thirteenth-century Paris school, especially in some of the windows of Nôtre Dame, just that hue was deliberately used, and is not the result, as some writers have contended, of the optical mixture of red and blue glass. The 'Gothic' world of Viollet-le-Duc was apparently full of antagonistic forces: vaults pushing and thrusting against one another, buttresses counterthrusting, colors encroaching, invading and being repulsed—all in dynamic opposition and reaction. Again and again his writings employ the words *lutter, combattre*, etc., etc. Such a perilous condition demands controls, countermeasures, and above all, system, and it is here that Viollet-le-Duc's 'rationalism' was applied with full force, restoring order and equilibrium and subordinating all things to physical law. We are already familiar with the thoroughgoing application of these 'laws' to the fields of architecture and stained glass, but in accordance with his passion for consistency he also applied his physical laws to the art of painting, providing us at the same time with an insight into his opinions of certain French artists who were not conforming to established conventions. This was written in the 1860s: 'But if painting is part of an ensemble, if it enters into the total harmony offered to our eyes by the entire structure, it is necessary to submit to purely physical laws which one cannot disregard and which are superior to talent or to the genius of the artist. Indeed, the genius of a master cannot modify the laws of light, of perspective, and of optics. We know well that a considerable number of artists of our time are characterized by spirits too fiery or independent to submit to laws other than those dictated by their fantasy; but we know with no less certainty that light, optics, and perspective, with their respective laws, cannot be modified to accommodate these unruly attitudes. . . . The artists who created the windows of the twelfth century demonstrated to the contrary, their absolute submission to these laws . . .'[18]

A curious indifference to style is revealed in another passage in which Viollet-le-Duc discusses an early thirteenth-century head from Saint-Rémi at Reims. (See overleaf.) 'At a distance of twenty meters, this head, so harshly delineated, takes on an entirely different character. Now we see the features of a young man with a soft beard . . . the right eyebrow is softened by the

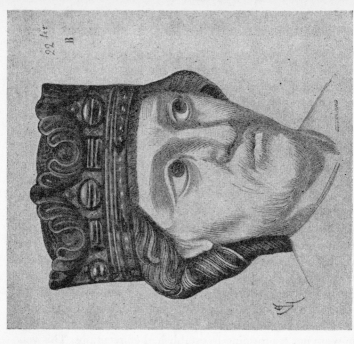

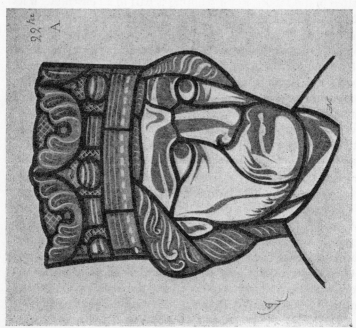

Two drawings of a head from Saint-Rémi, Reims (Viollet-le-Duc, *Vitrail*, pp. 421–2)
As seen close by
As seen from a distance

light area penetrating the dark. The mouth seems to be modelled with a softness quite juvenile, as well as the chin . . . [etc.]'[19] This interpretation would be surprising indeed to an artist of the Middle Ages who had not yet received the benefit of Beaux-arts instruction. Actually, in the panels at Chartres, the faces which contain such heavily loaded features are usually nineteenth-century restorations, e.g., those of Mary and the Angel in the *Annunciation* panel.[20]

Another example of repainting is furnished by the unfortunate moonfaced Child in the *Glorification* scene crowning the central window (Fig. 4), obviously an inept restoration. What little original facial painting remains in the west windows of Chartres is often delicate, without the broad, opaque strokes so frequently associated with this style, but it is impossible to say here that either method dominated glass painting in France at this time, for other schools varied considerably, the late twelfth-century ateliers of Bourges and Poitiers, for example, using a bold delineation which Viollet-le-Duc seems to associate with too extensive a period and locale.[21]

More readily seen is the famous *Belle Verrière* (Fig. 5), now closer to the viewer in its present location on the south wall of the ambulatory, its magnificent twelfth-century reds and blues in the center panels quite perfectly preserved. Unfortunately, the faces are from a later period, but the exquisite blue of the Virgin's robe is almost entirely original, along with the glass of the brilliant ruby background. Here again, we see no drawing or hatching on the blue areas adjacent to the reds to 'prevent the encroaching' of one color onto another, nor, at least to this observer's eyes, does there appear to be any unpleasant discoloration along the contiguous areas. Indeed, in all the twelfth-century glass of Chartres Cathedral there seems to be little evidence to support this particular contention of Viollet-le-Duc.

The author of *Vitrail* tends to minimize or ignore the variety and invention of this art, making few distinctions between the regional schools, their characteristic styles and colors, and the inevitable changes occurring from time to time. Grouped together are examples of stained glass from various periods and places, united apparently by the observance of laws and principles accounting for their excellence. Rarely does one encounter a concept of style, for example, without some justification in physical or material necessity, an attitude familiar to anyone acquainted with Viollet-le-Duc's architectural theories. Throughout the *Dictionnaire* and his other essays there recurs an insistence upon the principle of laws particular to and within the *métier*, with little tolerance for free association and interchange between the various arts. Reflecting the scientific spirit of his time, the 'rationalism' of Viollet-le-Duc attempted to organize and interpret the arts on a logical and systematic basis, allowing for few inconsistencies, and within this framework a remarkable edifice was created.

Serious scholarly questioning of the principles of *Vitrail* has never appeared, to my knowledge, except in a few cogent passages in Heinrich Oidtmann's treatise published in the latter part of the nineteenth century.[22] While, in general, Oidtmann has high praise for Viollet-le-Duc and his *Dictionnaire*, including the section on stained glass, he is critical of several points, including the French author's explanation for the heavy painting on the Saint-Rémi head. From his own observations, Oidtmann disagrees with the observation that the heavy lines and leading are transformed into nineteenth-century modeling, stating that they are still visible at the distance of twenty meters.[23] Also from the standpoint of personal observation, the German author takes exception to Viollet-le-Duc's contention that the color blue has a tendency to invade neighbouring tones, reporting that his observations in churches at Strasbourg, Walburg, and others, have been otherwise.[24] Finally, with respect to the use of white and beaded lines, Oidtmann reminds us that this device of separating colors is not peculiar to stained glass, but has been a common practice in many branches of painting.[25] Subsequent writing on stained glass has apparently taken little notice of these observations.

Using the *Tree of Jesse* window as a supreme example, Viollet-le-Duc, in a lengthy exposition, presents it as the embodiment and summation of those principles honored by the twelfth-century glass worker. He points to the painting on the draperies, the use of pearling in many places, and the lavish ornamentation of the borders as effective devices to control the irradiation of the blue ground. One passage in this section

causes me to wonder if Viollet-le-Duc ever saw this glass close
at hand, for he describes this blue as a limpid blue, slightly
tinged with green.[26] Actually, this is a perfect description of
the blue of the Jesse window when seen from the floor level of
the nave, especially at the crossing, but in reality the basic
background color of this window is of an entirely different
order. I shall never forget the first time I mounted the scaffolds
at Chartres to see these windows as close range: I was aston-
ished at the richness and depth of the colors, most of them
heavily saturated, *foncées*. The blue serving as the unifying
ground for all three windows is not limpid, but a deep, intense
blue, a cerulean blue of high saturation and low brilliance.[27]
The apparent desaturation of this color when seen from the
nave of the Cathedral—especially from the crossing—is caused
by a combination of factors which we shall discuss in an appropriate section. The *bleu limpide* mentioned by Viollet-le-Duc
does indeed occur in the west windows of Chartres, but only
in very limited areas, restricted to the robes of the most sacred
personages, appearing especially in the vestments of Christ and
the Virgin Mary. It is an extraordinarily beautiful blue, a *bleu
du ciel*, light, celestial, which I have encountered only in
twelfth-century glass, and then only rarely.[28] The robe of the
Virgin in the *Nativity* and *Presentation* scenes is of this color,
as is the garment of the Christ Child in the *Adoration* and
Glorification panels, and the robe of the Virgin in *La Belle
Verrière* is also shown in this color. This celestial blue is one of
the supreme moments in medieval art, for it is seemingly without body or substance, composed entirely of light. Weightless,
ethereal, it is matter transformed. The fragility and lightness
of its appearance is further enhanced by the contrasting ground
of intense and powerful reds, assertive and bold, opposed to
the delicacy of the blue. However, when the windows are seen
from a distance it seems that this divine color permeates the
entire ensemble, emanating, as it were, from the Supreme Light
to the lesser lights, transforming all things. Close at hand, however, at a distance from which they normally are never seen,
the windows are dominated by intense background colors,
especially the deep blue.

For all his allegiance to '*les lois de la lumière et de l'optique*,'

Viollet-le-Duc has some highly individual and arbitrary views along these lines, and one wonders if he was really very well acquainted with the optical theories of his time. Certainly his views concerning the distinctive irradiating power of blue, without qualification as to brightness or any other determining factors, have no bases in accepted scientific theory—then or now. In his discussion of various colors, separately or in combination, one senses that he regards them as independent physical phenomena, operating without the mediation of the *eye*, much in the same manner as he presents his architectural theories, with the visual sensibilities receiving very little accommodation.

One is puzzled concerning the source of Viollet-le-Duc's color theories. The nineteenth century produced many scientific and quasi-scientific theories on color (for it was a period of intense interest and investigation in this area) from the publication of Goethe's *Farbenlehre* in the early part of the century to the contributions of Chevreul, Fresnel, Von Helmholtz, Dobrowolsky, Maxwell, and many others. The monumental *Handbuch der physiologischen Optik* by Von Helmholtz first appeared in a complete edition in 1866, but had been earlier issued in sections in 1856, 1860, and 1866. In his preface to the first complete edition, the distinguished scientist speaks of the study of optics as 'this youthful . . . and effervescing field of knowledge . . ." A French edition translated by Javal and Klein, *Optique physiologique*, appeared in Paris in 1867, one year before the publication of the last volume of the *Dictionnaire* containing the article *Vitrail*. Viollet-le-Duc would have encountered in the German work—especially in the sections dealing with irradiation and chromatic aberrations of the eye— many facts which would have modified his own absolute laws.

At the heart of Viollet-le-Duc's stained glass theories is the optical phenomenon of irradiation, which was the subject of an important study by the Belgian physicist, Joseph Plateau, published in 1838, [29] which received wide notice in other European countries, especially in France and Germany. Plateau enlarges upon the basic principles of Galileo[30] which state that irradiation increases as the surrounding field becomes darker, and that it seems to amplify a light object seen on a dark ground. Plateau makes further observations:

> Irradiation increases with the length of contemplation of the object.
>
> With the same individual and for an object of the same brightness, irradiation varies considerably from one day to another.
>
> The average irradiation developed by the same brightness will be very different from one individual to another.[31]

As to the cause for this spreading of light, Plateau believed that 'the excitation produced by the light spreads over the retina a little beyond the contour of the image,' acknowledging his debt to Descartes who proposed the same theory in the seventeenth century.[32]

Von Helmholtz, agreeing with the observations of Plateau, contributes the following ideas: 'Irradiation can be explained by the fact that the intensity of the light sensation is not proportional to the objective intensity of the light. . . . The fundamental thing about all these appearances is that the edges of bright areas in the field of view are, as it were, shifted and tend to encroach on the adjacent darker areas. This encroachment is proportionately more and more noticeable as the accommodation becomes more inexact, at which point the blurred circles projected into the eye from each point of the bright area get bigger and bigger.'[33]

Thus far we have spoken more in terms of the irradiation of light rather than the irradiation of its component colors. The perception of color is complicated by the fact that the eye has different focal lengths for light of different colors, as Fraunhofer and Von Helmholtz observed by the 1860s,[34] producing under certain conditions effects of blurring and erratic focus, although normally the eye makes such quick adjustments that we are unaware of these differences in color refraction within the eye. There is little reason to believe, however, that one color, as such, has a greater tendency to spread than another color, but this would certainly occur if that color were appreciably *brighter* than adjacent colors, containing (or letting through) a greater *amount* of light. Therefore, especially in the case of transparent or translucent color, any spectral hue could irradiate more than the others if it exceeded them in brightness. In an equal energy spectrum, for example, the central area containing the yellows and light-greens is the brightest; it is these colors, rather than the blues or reds, that seem to overflow themselves.

An early twentieth-century writer on stained glass, Lewis F. Day, seems to sense this intuitively as he discusses the problems of painting on glass: 'Something, however, had to be done to prevent especially the whites, yellows, and pale blues, and in some degree all but the dark colors, from taking more than their due part in the general effect, and this was accomplished by increased patterning on the light areas.'[35] Following this, he writes: 'Viollet-le-Duc endeavours to explain with scientific precision which are the colours which spread most, and how they spread. His analysis is useful as well as interesting, but absolute definition of the effect of radiation is possible only with regard to a rigidly fixed range of colours to which no colourist would ever confine himself. A man gets by experience to know the value of his colours in their place, and thinks out his scheme accordingly. He puts, as a matter of course, more painting into pale draperies than into dark, and so on; but to a great extent he acts upon that subtle sort of reasoning which we call feeling. Intuition it may be, but it is the intuition of a man who knows.'[36]

Closer to Viollet-le-Duc's own time, however, were the studies of the great Viennese anatomist and physiologist, Ernst Brücke, who published his book on color in 1866, an influential work published in both German and French editions.[37] Brücke saw no difficulties in the combination of red and blue, and considered them a good combination, since they are complementary or approximately complementary colors.[38] Observing the difference in retinal accommodation for these colors in stained glass, he says: 'When looking from a certain distance at multicolored windows made up of red and blue squares encased in black framework, it seems that the reds are nearer than the blues, and that they stand out; the black areas, formed by the armatures, appear to be oblique planes leading to the more distant blues. The inverse of this I have never observed. The advancing colors are: red, orange, and yellow; the receding colors belong to the diverse categories of blue.'[39]

Brücke admits that most of the ideas and observations in his book are subjective, and he is much more hesitant than Viollet-le-Duc in the formulation of optical 'laws' and 'principles.' In his preliminary qualifications for a chapter on color juxtaposition, Brücke remarks, 'Up to the present time I have not been able to discover a general law, including all cases which we are going to consider; those [laws] which others have sought to establish do not seem to me to be sufficiently justified. Rules which pertain to certain pairs of colors and not to others do not deserve to be called laws.'[40]

Brücke was the son of Johannes Gottfried Brücke, a painter and Professor of Anatomy at Berlin's Akademie der Künste. In the preface to his book he writes of long association with artists and critics, expressing the intention to complete and publish a study on the connection between optics and the arts, which was later realized as the *Bruchstücke aus der Theorie der bildenden Künste*,[41] translated into French the following year in an edition which included an essay on optics and painting by Von Helmholtz.[42] In their studies, the nineteenth-century scientists are reluctant to proclaim absolute laws in the field of color, devoting their attention rather to a series of careful experiments and sensitive observations which display them to better advantage in fields outside their own than we have observed in the case of the architect-archaeologist who undertakes to invade the sciences. Curiously, in spite of the fact that they were turned in the other's direction, there is little evidence of reciprocal influence or exchange of experimental data between them, although the scientists show much greater awareness and sensitivity in the arts than the French author reveals in the sciences. There is apparently no connection between their works, and we must turn in other directions in our attempt to find the possible sources for the stained glass theories of Viollet-le-Duc.

Perhaps the most influential French writer on color during the nineteenth century was the amazing Michel Eugène Chevreul (1786–1889), who lived to the age of 103, publishing many articles and books on this subject from 1807 to the end of his life. Chevreul, chemist to the Gobelin factory, was another example of the nineteenth-century scientist widely conversant in the arts, and of considerable influence in its theory and literature, and, toward the end of the nineteenth century, in its practice, especially in the hands of the Neo-Impressionists. His Gobelin lectures on simultaneous contrast were delivered during the years 1836–1838, coming out in book form the following year.[43] Over 200 articles flowed from his pen, devoted especially to problems of color, including studies in stained glass in which he was careful to distinguish between color contrasts and color mixtures, and also between the phenomena of reflected and transmitted light, the latter in both cases applying more particularly to the stained glass medium.[44] It is surprising that there is little correspondence between the theories of Chevreul and his equally prominent contemporary, Viollet-le-Duc, for the activities of both men were well known and their publications widely read. But the writings of Chevreul contain no hint of perilous contrasts between red and blue, nor does he regard one color as more aggressive than any other. On the contrary, he points out that strongly contrasting colors like red and blue usually strengthen and enhance each other.[45] In direct contrast to Viollet-le-Duc's anxiety about encroaching colors in stained glass, Chevreul observes: 'Colored windows appear to me to produce all the effect of which they are really capable only in a vast edifice where the differently colored rays arrive at the eye of the spectator on the floor of the church, so scattered by the effect of the conical figure of the rays of light emanating from a single point, that they impinge upon each other, whence results an harmonious mixture, which is not found in a small structure lighted by stained windows.[46]

On the basis of these views, therefore, it is difficult to subscribe to the opinions expressed by some modern stained glass artists that perhaps Chevreul was possibly the author of *Vitrail*, for there seems to be little relationship between him and Viollet-le-Duc, either in general principles or in detailed observations of translucent light.

Whatever the source of Viollet-le-Duc's color theories, it apparently will not be found in the serious scientific literature of the nineteenth century. We must look in other directions, but before we do this it will be useful to recall for a few moments an interesting critique of his methodology and of his personal attitudes by a late-nineteenth-century biographer, Anthyme

Saint-Paul, who comments on Viollet-le-Duc's predilection for '... opinions too quickly formed and too narrowly grouped into systems ...'[47] Of the man himself, he says, 'The great stumbling block for him was his presumption, his confidence in his own opinion, his disdain of all counsel, inexcusable traits for even the greatest geniuses...'[48] Saint-Paul, writing two years after the death of Viollet-le-Duc, points out that the latter reacted to criticism as a personal affront, and then would accuse his critics of being antagonistic to archaeology and even to reason itself.[49] (This biographer was one of the first to question one of the most famous theories of the *Dictionnaire* concerning the rise of the Gothic style in which the ribbed vault was regarded as a prime form-giver to this architecture.)

While French and German color theories offer little precedent for the positive assertions and 'laws' of Viollet-le-Duc, there existed in another country a thriving number of colorists highly honored in their time and vastly influential in their own and other countries. Victorian England suffered no lack of authoritative texts on matters of color harmony and decoration, from the early writings of George Field to the later admonitions of Ruskin and Charles Eastlake, for, in the words of one of these writers, John Wilkinson, 'In no country is the cultivation of taste more necessary than in England.' These colorists and arbiters of taste, setting out to correct this situation, wrote books on art and decoration bearing little or no relationship to the distinguished researches in optics and color by fellow countrymen like Newton and Maxwell, scientists whose pronouncements on color harmony were much less arbitrary and assured.

As early as 1817, George Field spoke of colors belonging to 'an universal archetype,' and organized his system according to a scale extending from black to white.[50] In the 1858 edition of *Chromatics*, Field offers numerical ratios for mixing primary hues to obtain a harmonious effect: it is called *The Scale of Equivalents*, and consists of three parts of yellow, five of red, and eight of blue. In this manner, they are said to 'neutralize each other ... numbered according to the relative and opposed power with which they accord, contrast, and harmonize each other in mixture.'[51]

Field's color principles were echoed at mid-century by 'the greatest ornamentist of modern times,' Owen Jones (1809–1874), whose *Grammar of Ornament*[52] was one of the most influential publications of its kind, and was received enthusiastically both in England and on the Continent, where it subsequently appeared in French and German editions. Jones was an interior decorator, but of such distinction and fame that he once served as President of the Royal Institute of British Architects, receiving from this organization a gold medal for his distinguished work; he also received a medal from the Paris World's Fair of 1867. Perhaps his most important undertaking was in connection with the interior decoration of the Crystal Palace in 1851, for which he prescribed the color scheme employed on the structural membering. Jones was also in charge of the Fine Arts Exhibit for this exposition, lavishing particular attention on a reproduction of the *Casa Reál* from the Alhambra, which embodied, according to Jones, many of the true principles of successful coloring. Popular reception to his decoration was considerable, for according to contemporaries witnessing the opening of the Crystal Palace in 1851, 'It was universally felt that a new era in decorative art had commenced in England.'[53] Further, his obituary notice says that 'It would be impossible to mention the name of any one whose genius and taste combined have had greater influence on the decorative arts of this country than that of Mr. Owen Jones.'[54]

Concerning the principles contributing to the beauty of the Alhambra, Owen Jones says: 'An examination of the *Casa Reál*, and even our own reproduction, will show how perfectly the Moors regarded what we hold to be the first principle in architecture—*to decorate construction, never to construct decoration*: in Moorish architecture not only does the decoration arise naturally from the construction, but the constructive idea is carried out in every detail of the ornamentation of the surface.'[55] This was written at mid-century, and Viollet-le-Duc published his article, *Construction*, about five years later.

For the proper control of the primary colors—red, blue, and gold—which dominate the decorative scheme, Jones had the following directions: 'The several colours are either separated by white bands, or by the shadow caused by the relief of the ornament itself—and this appears to be an absolute principle required in colouring—*colours should never be allowed to impinge upon each other.*[56] Moreover, if the colors are applied in proper proportion according to Field's ratios, a pleasing effect would result which Jones calls 'a neutralized bloom.'[57]

Thirty-seven principles or 'propositions' for correct coloring are set forth in the sumptuous 1856 edition of *The Grammar of Ornament* which covers the history of the decorative arts from 'savage tribes' to eighteenth-century France. Several of the propositions follow:

15. When ornaments in a colour are on a ground of a contrasting colour, the ornament should be separated from the ground by an edging of lighter colour,—as a red flower on a green ground should have an edging of lighter red.
16. When ornaments in a colour are on a gold ground the ornaments should be separated from the ground by an edging of a darker colour.
17. Gold ornaments on any coloured ground should be outlined with black.
18. Ornaments of any colour may be separated from grounds of any other colour by edgings of white, gold or black.[58]

In their designations of primary and secondary colors, the systems of Jones and Viollet-le-Duc are quite similar: blue, yellow, and red for the primaries; with light purple, emerald green, turquoise blue-green, etc., belonging to the 'composite' or *'couleurs composées'* variety.[59] Primaries are to be employed in larger areas and secondary colors in smaller details. Only on one major principle does Jones differ from Viollet-le-Duc—his belief that it is the color red which has a tendency to overpower other colors. All of the propositions of Jones are based, of course, on opaque, reflected surfaces, especially as applied to the Crystal Palace, a monument which could not have failed to excite the interest of the great Frenchman. Viollet-le-Duc, moreover, was an honorary member and correspondent of the Royal Institute of British Architects.[60]

When *The Grammar of Ornament* was published on the Continent, it came to the attention of Brücke, who said that although some of the propositions frequently coincided with artistic practice he could not accept the totality of these laws. Brücke devotes only a few passages to Jones' ideas, admitting

that he is mentioning him at all only because of 'the considera-
tion which he enjoys.'[61]

A friend and admirer of Owen Jones, Sir John Wilkinson,
makes specific comments on the art of stained glass in his book,
*On Colour and on the Necessity for a General Diffusion of
Taste Among All Classes.*[62]

Another error, greatly to be condemned, is the confusion sometimes seen
in blues and reds, which are made to appear purple when seen at a distance. It has been fatal to many of our modern windows, otherwise not
devoid of merit. Among the causes of this are the want of a sufficient
quantity of yellow, the improper arrangement of the reds and blues, and
the absence of other colours required to combine with them. A yellow, or
a white, fillet between the red and blue, or a spot of the same placed on
the centre, or at the junction of the two, will obviate it . . .[63]

Wilkinson cites the use of this device in the windows of
Saint-Denis.

Concerning figure painting on medieval glass, Wilkinson has
this to say:

. . . We are not bound to imitate the faulty drawing or the inelegance of
the figures of an early period. Had the designers of those days been able
to draw them well, they would have done so; incapacity, not choice, com-
pelled them to make them faulty and rude, and we are not, therefore,
bound to copy them in this particular.[64]

This was ten years before the publication of *Vitrail*.

In addition to this curious similarity between the theories of
Viollet-le-Duc and the writings of English decorators, there
appears to be a kinship in their common disregard for accepted
scientific data produced by careful and cautious experimenta-
tion. Apparently, they preferred to make their own rules, exer-
cising their passion for order and authority by formulating
rigid systems of laws and principles in which uncertainty was
never allowed to intrude, least of all in the uncertain field of
color. If they had any doubts, they did not express them.
Rather, in reading their authoritative pronouncements, one is
impressed by an unshakeable confidence in the correctness of
their own ideas.

Viollet-le-Duc, particularly in his 'rationalist' theories,
seemed to confuse the causal and teleological explanations of
science, blending his phenomenological observations with post-

facto rationalization to explain the use of certain elements in the windows.[65] Many devices like the beading and pearling of borders, the use of strips, etc., are there, in all likelihood, to enhance the general visual richness of the windows; it is highly questionable whether the medieval glazier was unduly concerned with the problem of controlling the blues—or any other color, for that matter.

On the other hand, if Viollet-le-Duc saw violet fringes while looking at blue glass for any length of time, we cannot argue with him, for it is possible that violet was the color he actually perceived. Among the vast differences in the reactions of individuals to certain colors (in addition to various forms of color blindness, protanopia in particular), is one known as the 'phenomenon of decay,' in which some observers report that certain blues turn violet after retinal adaptation of twenty to forty seconds.[66] This phenomenon of decay often occurs along with a loss of saturation in the color contemplated. We can only surmise, therefore, that this might have been the physiological response of the French author.

Still with us, however, is the generally accepted optical phenomenon in the nave of Chartres that the west windows seem to lose their red coloration and become predominantly blue when seen from a distance. Can this be attributed to the Purkinje phenomenon? (See Chapter I.) We must be cautious here, for, while a partial dark-adaptation takes place when one is inside the Cathedral for any length of time, causing some loss of acuity and a moderate heightening of the blues, the radical change observed in the west windows may also be seen (perhaps not as vividly) by a person just entering the Cathedral with light-adapted eyes, and may also be recorded in a color photograph taken from the crossing, which will come out predominantly blue.

Not unimportant in accounting for this phenomenon is the disarmingly simple fact that more blue glass is used in these windows than any other color, and this seems to establish the character of the total ensemble. When all the translucent colors are seen from a distance, moreover, they combine in the eye in an additive mixture which in its totality is less saturated than the component hues—in contrast to subtractive combinations of opaque, surface colors which become darker as they are mixed together.[67]

At the same time, one notices in the thirteenth-century windows of the same Cathedral (e.g., the south transept rose and many of the clerestory windows—also dominated by red and blue glass), that these ensembles do not show the same overall blue tonality when seen from a distance. Instead, the reds seem to hold their own, and do not melt into a lighter blue-dominated ensemble as did their twelfth-century counterparts. One reason for this might be the smaller size of the individual fragments of glass in the older window—jewel-like pieces throughout— which would fuse more readily at a distance; another reason is related to the fact that the thirteenth-century reds are generally more heavily saturated than the twelfth-century examples. According to spectophotometric analyses of both types done at the Case Institute of Technology in Cleveland, the color curve of the earlier reds inclines much more to the orange wavelengths, while the thirteenth-century reds belong to the extreme red end of the spectrum. In an additive color mixture, therefore, the reds nearest the center of the spectrum will blend more readily with the other hues, resulting in a color which is the sum of all the component wavelengths, but, because it is an addition of lights, it will be of lighter saturation than the component hues.

My hypothesis for the unassertive carrying power of the reds in the west windows, in addition to the reasons already given, will be developed in the next chapter by an examination of their internal structure which distinguishes them from other colors in use during this period.

CHAPTER III

THE GLASS

CENTURIES of weathering have deposited a heavy patina on the exterior surfaces of twelfth- and thirteenth-century stained glass panels, contributing in no small measure to the light-resistant qualities of this material. In addition to surface coating, the inner structure of old glass is dense and complicated, broken up by impurities, bubbles, streaks and unequal color distribution, rendering this glass a deeply translucent medium in contrast to the transparency encountered in many examples of modern stained glass. Even without its surface patina, old glass would still be more translucent than transparent, chiefly due to the irregularities and complexities within the body of the material.

It is erroneous to assume, however, that clear, transparent glass could not be produced in the Middle Ages. An examination of existing specimens of vitreous ware from the Roman period onward will refute this idea. Authors as early as Pliny record that 'the highest value is set upon glass that is entirely colorless and transparent, as nearly as possible resembling crystal . . .'[1] Many glass objects have acquired a surface iridescence in the intervening years which they did not possess originally, but there are still preserved in such collections as the Corning Museum, and other museums in America and Europe, a variety of drinking vessels and decorative objects which appear to the eye as clearer and more evenly transparent than the stained glass we are discussing, although they would not rate very high according to modern optical standards.

One often hears the opinion that old windows were probably as glaring as modern examples when they were first installed, that the action of weather over the years has had an enriching effect upon them, an effect which today has to be approximated by the use of matt, a semi-opaque vitreous paint applied to over-bright areas of modern windows. While the accidental but beneficial effects of weather cannot be denied, there are indications that conscious efforts were made by the medieval glassmaker to enrich his medium before surface coatings were

E

applied either by man or by nature, and these efforts are revealed especially in the reds, or 'rubies,' of the period we are discussing. In order to appreciate the structure of these earlier reds, it might be interesting to compare them with their modern counterparts. As an illustration, let us compare a twelfth-century red from Chartres with an 'antique' ruby in present-day use. (In modern glass terminology, 'antique' glass is that material which is hand-blown, and therefore more irregular than commercial rolled glass. The chief sources for 'antique' glass are in Europe, especially in Germany.)

Under a high-powered microscope, these modern and medieval reds present vastly different structures which ordinarily are not apparent to the naked eye. Through the cooperation of specialists in microphotography it has been possible to record these differences on film.[2] (See Figs. 6 and 7.)

Figure 6 shows the magnified edge of the modern red. It is 5 mm. in thickness, and lined on one side (the upper part in the photograph) with a thin coating of vitreous red which gives this piece its dominant color. Most of the thickness of the example is made up of clear, colorless glass, as revealed in the photograph. The vitreous lining is acquired during a glass-blowing operation in which the cylinder of clear molten glass is dipped in a red 'pot'-metal that fuses as a thin film over its surface, becoming permanently fixed as the cylinder is cut and cooled. This procedure differs from older 'flashing' methods in its application of the red coating *after* the cylinder has been blown, a contrast to traditional practice in which the component layers are gathered on the blowpipe before the cylinder is formed.[3]

In Figure 7, the 3 mm. edge of the twelfth-century Chartres fragment reveals a marked difference in the proportioning of the red area (the upper section in the photograph) and the colorless (actually, green-tinted) area, for here the pigmented layer occupies approximately half the thickness of the glass. To the naked eye the pigmented half appears to be a solid color, but under the microscope it presents an extraordinary sight, a highly complex structure composed of many thin laminations of red alternating with striae of colorless glass, totaling as many as fifty-six laminae in certain sections of this fragment. It is impossible to make a precise count which would apply to the entire piece, for it will be noticed that the red striae (white lines in the photograph) often fuse with one another, sometimes blending, other times separating, and occasionally tapering off altogether. Additional obstacles to microscopic observation are presented by the chips and pits on the surface of the glass, and even by a speck of dust (the white, hook-shaped object on the left, overlapping the two areas) which settled on the piece during the photographing. Nevertheless, the magnification of this twelfth-century fragment shows it to be an exceedingly complicated and irregular medium in contrast to the uniformity of the modern example, and the photograph also reveals a fluid transition between the layers of the older piece, the result of flashing the component colors before the blowing operation was begun.

How were these microscopic laminations produced in this twelfth-century red? Unfortunately we do not have a definitive answer to this problem, although several theories have been advanced. The French scientist, Chesneau, has made chemical analyses of twelfth- and thirteenth-century stained glass samples from Châlons-sur-Marne, Amiens, and Reims, and in addition has recorded observations of selected fragments, especially the reds, under the microscope.[4] M. Chesneau suggests that successive gatherings were made from alternate pots, after which the metal was spun out by centrifugal force in the manner of crown glass, a method he describes as *soufflage en plat, plateau,* or *en boudines* (other French writers refer to it as *en cives*). As further evidence of crown glass technique, M. Chesneau points to the elliptical shape of the air bubbles in both the red and colorless layers of his samples. Moreover, he contends that the attenuated striae are the result of the rapid and forceful movement caused by the spinning of the blowpipe.

Dr. Jane Hayward, who is at work on the American section of the *Corpus Vitrearum Medii Aevi,* makes the following suggestion: colorless and red glass were added with care to the same pot, with the red on top of the colorless. The pot was then stirred slightly so that some of the colorless glass was 'marbled' through the red. The pipe was then dipped the full depth of the pot and raised slowly. The gathering was then blown and spun by the crown method. This would explain the underlay of colorless and the overlay of striated red. It would also account for the fact that the surfaces of many fragments of twelfth- and thirteenth-century red glass are only partially colored, with large white areas present.

An interesting article has appeared in the *Journal of the Society of Glass Technology*, which, although not directly related to the stained glass of the Middle Ages, suggests another possible method for producing multiple laminations in ruby glass. The author, Henry John Tress, reports on an experiment in which 'recurrent layers were formed in ruby glasses by the folding to and fro of a falling ribbon of molten glass when poured into a mould. ... The outside of a falling ribbon of glass undergoes chilling, evaporation, oxidation, and surface adsorption; further, the pot-metal may not be quite homogeneous. These differences render layering visible in the finished glass. The layers reveal themselves in clear glasses, particularly those containing lead oxide, by slight variations in refractive index; marked variations of opalescence and colour occur in those glasses which strike on cooling.'[5] Considerable research must still be done before we come to a satisfactory solution of this problem. One American glass artist, Lawrence Saint, who has done windows for the National Cathedral in Washington and the Swedenborgian church in Bryn Athyn, Pennsylvania, has used glass of his own manufacture which has been inspired by medieval prototypes. Of this glass, the reds I have seen possess thin laminations of colored material running through the colorless, but they are widely separated by larger areas of colorless glass between them. They appear to be made by the single-pot method described by Dr. Hayward.

The Chartres piece we have examined is apparently representative of other reds from this period, for Chesneau has encountered flashed rubies dating from the twelfth and thirteenth centuries at Saint-Rémi, Reims, Châlons-sur-Marne, and Amiens which show a variety of stratification patterns, some containing more laminations than others, and in different arrangements, but all bearing witness to an experimental and purposeful effort on the part of the medieval artist to control the color and enrich the quality of light in his windows. Chesneau suggests that the blower could add the red in successive layers until he obtained the desired tint, which would be feasible if the two-pot method proposed by Chesneau were followed. Whatever the procedure, the medieval artist succeeded in creating a complex structure which allowed only a fraction of incident light to penetrate his medium, a medium that scattered the rays again and again in a complicated implosion producing the vibrancy and richness normally associated with old glass, giving it a quality of glowing from within, the *Eigenlicht* described by Wolfgang Schöne in his recent *Über das Licht in der Malerei*.

The apparent lack of carrying power of the reds in the west windows of Chartres may be partly explained, therefore, by their complicated inner structure which interferes with the passage of light, diffusing it and scattering the rays in many directions, perhaps to a greater extent than the interference within the blues and other colors not microscopically laminated. Otherwise the various colors are similar in their imperfection and irregularity of material and in the amount of weathering on their surfaces.[6]

Are there any precedents for this special technique in ruby glass? Is it peculiar to the stained glass art, or is it related in some manner to techniques practiced in other fields? Certain indications point to the arts of the goldsmith, not in connection with the working of precious metals and jewels, essentially, but in the imitation of precious stones in glass, one of the oldest and most popular uses for this material.

For centuries a superficial relationship between the art of stained glass and the art of imitating precious stones has been acknowledged, arising in part from the use of a common vocabulary—it having been the custom of medieval and modern glassworkers to describe various colors according to the jewels they most closely resembled—and again by frequent poetic allusions to the 'jewel-like' quality of old glass which have appeared, not without justification, in the accounts of scholars and laymen.[7] On the basis of more specialized and technical information from the field of gemmology, however, it may be possible to inquire into this relationship with greater thoroughness, for numerous analyses of imitation gems by experts have suggested a more than superficial connection between these arts.

In general, the two are united in their search for brilliance and beauty of color, and in their preference for translucent rather than transparent media. The desire in stained glass to increase the vibrancy and richness of windows is curiously paralleled by the effort in jewelry to simulate the high dispersive powers of precious stones. During the Middle Ages these objectives were subtly fused.

Jean Escard's microscopic studies of artificial rubies invite comparison with similar features in ruby glass of early Gothic windows.[8] In Plate XXIII, Figure 4, of his book (see Fig. 8 in this work) Escard reveals minute striation patterns and bubbles within the body of the artificial gem which resemble the linear configurations in early types of flashed ruby found at Chartres and Amiens. The striae, as in stained glass examples, vary considerably within the piece, tapering and fusing in a fluid pattern (in contrast to the crystalline structure of genuine stones), with a scattering of bubbles, often elliptical in shape, distributed throughout the mass. Escard does not discuss the origin or source of these artificial rubies, but they undoubtedly belong to one of the nineteenth-century types created by synthetic processes developed by Gaudin, Verneuil, and others, in which small particles of genuine rubies were reduced to powder and fused with chemicals at high temperatures to produce a stone similar to the genuine ruby in all its natural properties save for the striations and bubbles revealed under the microscope.[9] This nineteenth-century process is a more refined and scientific development of an older art which from ancient times has been practiced chiefly in glassmaking.

Among the many techniques used to simulate precious stones is the popular device known to jewellers as the 'doublet,' a composite form lending itself to a variety of combinations and materials.[10] Basically, the doublet is a cut stone consisting of an upper and a lower portion cemented together to give the appearance of a single stone. When the two portions are of genuine stones, it is known as a 'genuine doublet,' but other combinations are possible, such as the 'semi-genuine doublet,' with one portion of genuine and the other portion of lesser

material, either semi-precious stone or glass. Of a lower order
is the 'false doublet,' made of one layer of colored and the other
of colorless material, with glass frequently used in one or both
portions; the 'hollow doublet,' of hollowed-out crystal filled
with colored glass, is another variety. These last categories
are of greater interest to us, for they recall the structure of
lined and flashed stained glass, that of ruby glass in particular.

It is undoubtedly a variation of the doublet which is described by the seventeenth-century gemmologist, Thomas
Nicols, in a passage on 'the Adulteration of the Carbuncle or
Ruby . . . by glewing two fair *Crystalls* together with a little
mastick tinctured with a red or crimson colour.'[11] In another
section, Nicols indicates that the *doublée* (as he calls it) was
fashioned by fusing two vitreous layers in the molten state: 'As
for other gemms which are dissembled with tinctured glasse,
these for the most part seem to have a *pellicula* or little film in
their superficies, as if they were anointed with oyl, which is
never to be found in true gemms. There are factitious gemms
made of Crystall, and of flints, and lead, which will be harder
than the common glasse, and transparent as Crystall; in the
making of which, to tincture them, cunning artists are wont to
adde metalls to it, or tinctures, or colours of metalls, and thus
they being committed to the fire, by the operation of the heat
upon them, will be produced a gemme scarcely to be discerned
from the true gemme, save only by the atomes in the middle
of their bodie, and by those small *bullae* which are often caused
in them by the unequall working of the fire upon their matter,
or by the extreme vehemence of its heat.'[12] It is apparent that
the process described by Nicols involves firing and coloring
with metallic oxides, and also includes mention of the *pellicula*,
the *atomes*, and the *bullae*, corresponding, respectively, to the
colored vitreous lining, the small foreign particles, and the
bubbles found in older examples of stained glass. Similar observations are found in one of the earliest printed books on the
art of glassmaking, *L'arte vetraria*, by Antonio Neri, published
in Florence in 1612.[13] This book is concerned almost entirely
with the preparation of metallic oxides and paste in imitation
of precious stones.

Turning for a moment to the criteria employed in distinguishing true from false gems, it is noteworthy that apart from the use of scientific instruments, the ancients observed quite the same standards in use today. A modern authority lists the following: refractive index, specific gravity, hardness, and thermal conductivity—genuine stones being colder to the touch. Moreover, imitation gems are opaque to X rays, and under the microscope 'generally show spherical bubbles and curved striae.'[14] Pliny the Elder, without any apparatus, arrived at similar conclusions: a true gem is told by its color, weight, 'coolness in the mouth,' and hardness, for it cannot be scratched 'by an iron,' an observation consistent with the Mohs scale in use today. Pliny (*Natural History*, xxxvii, 76) further asserts that imitations can be found out by 'blisters in the body of the fictitious stone . . . filaments . . . and an unequal brilliancy.' In Book xxxvi, 67, Pliny describes the use of glass in the making of many types of imitation gems. Special mention is made of rubies in another passage: 'They are counterfeited, too, with great exactness in glass . . . and they present small blisters within . . .' (Book xxxvii, 26).

In the sacred and alchemic literature of the Middle Ages, from the early *Mappae Clavicula* and *Compositiones ad tingenda*[15] to the artists' 'handbooks' of Theophilus and Heraclius, considerable attention is given to the fabrication of gems from glass, reflecting the importance of this art in connection with the arts of the jeweler and the goldsmith for the creation of a wide variety of objects for sacred and secular purposes. Echoes of Pliny occur frequently, interspersed with extracts from the folklore, wizardry, and chemistry of the Middle Ages.[16]

Theophilus is the best known among medieval writers on glass, devoting many sections of his famous *Schedula Diversarum Artium*[17] to the preparation of vitreous materials and colorants for glass vessels, enamels, colored windows, and imitation gems. This work reveals a complicated interrelationship between these arts, for it is often difficult to distinguish between procedures for one or for the other. As an example, in Book II, 12, 'Of Divers Colours of Glass, not transparent,' he suggests the re-use of ancient glass mosaics and vessels for 'coloured gems . . . costly plates of sapphire . . . and windows.'

When Theophilus speaks 'Of Placing Gems upon Painted Glass,' he is referring, of course, to *imitation* emeralds, hyacinths, sapphires and other jewels 'in figures upon windows, in crosses, books, or in ornament of draperies . . .' (Book II, 28). All through this work it is apparent that methods, as well as nomenclature and uses, are frequently interchangeable.

Medieval gems, both genuine and false, were usually fashioned *en cabochon*. A cabochon stone is smooth-surfaced, rounded, or oblong, without the brilliant faceted cutting employed on modern gems. The faceting of precious stones, especially the diamond, was first developed with scientific thoroughness during the Renaissance, when the plotting of tables and facets was characteristically determined by an orderly geometric schema which produced brilliant and glittering effects of directed light in contrast to the more subdued luminosity of a natural stone. In place of bright stabs of prismatic color flashing from multifaceted surfaces, the light of a cabochon jewel appears to abide within the body of the gem, hovering vaguely, elusively, suspended mysteriously in a shifting atmosphere of light and color. During the contemplation of such a medium, one is not conscious of external sources of illumination activating the body of the jewel; rather, it seems that the light is glowing from within, a belief not uncommon in the Middle Ages.

A method for the preparation of a glass cabochon is described in the writings of the medieval craftsman, Heraclius, in his *De coloribus et artibus Romanorum*.[18] Heraclius, like Theophilus, is frequently occupied with the creation of imitation gems. In Book I, 14, *De Gemmis quas de Romano vitro facere quaeris*, Heraclius gives instructions for the making of 'beautiful shining stones out of Roman glass,' directing that small pieces of glass be placed in a mold which is 'hollowed according to the form of the stone,' then the mass is heated and stirred, after which it is fired in an oven. An interesting refinement occurs in this section: during the firing process Heraclius advises the craftsman to press on the glass 'with a broad, even iron in order to avoid a bubble, or any other flaw.' In another passage, different methods for working glass are described: 'From the mass it is again melted and formed into a molten state, one by blowing, and another by turning with a turning iron, a third engraved like silver. One also colors it in different manners so that it imitates hyacinths, and green sapphire, onyx, and gems of other colors.' (Book III, 5.) Here, in apparent context with the preparation of glass gems, are the familiar techniques of cylinder and crown so closely associated with stained glass.[19] Throughout this work, such an association is suggested many times in passages intermingled with directions for a great variety of operations, including the engraving and polishing of precious and imitation stones, the preparation of gold, the simulation of gold and silver, and many other processes in which real and imitation, precious and nonprecious, are treated concurrently, united by the medieval preoccupation with the transmutation of metals and above all by an absorbing interest in a wide range of light-bearing objects which glow and radiate with an uncommon power. The rule played by these luminous materials in the religious practice and aesthetic attitudes of the Middle Ages is well known.[20]

Students of medieval art are aware that most of the gems on reliquaries, book-covers, and other objects in museums and cathedral treasuries are either semi-precious stones or glass, and that these lesser materials were not necessarily substituted at a later date—although this did occur—but in as many instances belonged to the piece in its original state. Apparently, in the majority of cases, no deception was intended: we, hear, however, of notable exceptions like the Sapphire of Queen Theodolinda in the Cathedral Treasury of Monza, or 'Charlemagne's Emerald' at Reichenau, both believed to be genuine until nineteenth-century research proved them to be glass.[21] On occasion, legal steps were taken to assure a distinction between the true and false: toward the middle of the fourteenth century, laws were passed regulating the guilds of the *cristalliers* and the *pierriers de voirre*—cutters of crystal and natural stones who were also skilled at fabrications—in order to avoid confusion between real and imitation stones.[22] Commercially, of course this distinction must always have been important, but for decorative purposes there was apparently no prejudice against substitutes if costlier materials were not available. In fact, the transformation of base materials into objects of brightness and color had a special appeal to the medieval mind; the revelation of potential luminosity in dull surfaces provided a favorite analogy for the Dionysian light metaphysics of the twelfth and thirteenth centuries, a period intoxicated with light in all its manifestations. These centuries, moreover, witnessed the development and perfection of the Gothic style, a style which brought together in complex interrelationship and rare concordance the sumptuous arts, the art of stained glass, and the art of architecture. Contributing in no small measure to the achievement of this harmony were the skills of the goldsmith and the versatility of the artisan in glass.[23]

As a cabochon jewel does not transmit directed rays of light —seeming rather to glow from within—so do ancient windows diffuse and transform the light of day into the 'new light' of the Celestial Jerusalem. They are the *selbstleuchtende Wände*, transforming the interior beauty of the Cathedral with transcendent light, removing the spectator from the natural world and lifting him up 'according to his capacity.' The windows, with their richness and depth of color, invite the contemplation and intoxication of the viewer as he is lured to explore the inner mysteries of light in precious stones. Both mediums, within the framework of the Dionysian light metaphysics of the Middle Ages, are perfect vehicles for mystical contemplation.

It is natural in this context that we think of Abbot Suger of Saint-Denis, who so justly is associated with the genesis of the Gothic Style and the development of the monumental art of stained glass. Nowhere is the love for shining objects and precious materials revealed with greater enthusiasm than in the writings of this key figure in church and kingdom.[24] His works abound in elaborate descriptions of altar frontals, sacred vessels, and richly decorated objects, especially those ornamented with precious stones, and it is in the contemplation of these luminous materials that he describes his famous *ascensio* (*De Administratione* XXXIII). In succeeding passages, Suger gives an elaborate account of his sumptuous and 'most sacred windows,' including those of sapphire glass, entrusted to the care of 'a master craftsman and a goldsmith.' (*De Administratione* XXXIV; *De Consecratione* IV). Coeval with, or perhaps a few years later than, the Saint-Denis windows were the west windows above the *Royal Portal* at Chartres. The connection between these two centers has long been recognized, and it is highly probable that workers and artists—as well as clerics— went frequently from one to the other. By their letters and activities we know of the friendship between Abbot Suger and Bishop Geoffrey of Chartres.[25]

Therefore, it is the technique of the jeweler that we encounter in the west windows of Chartres, for the methods of imitating precious stones and the preparation of glass for windows of this period are frequently similar, especially with reference to ruby glass. It is still an unexplained mystery, however, that red glass—both in paste jewelry and in windows—should be laminated while other colors at this time were generally homogeneous. Earlier it was stated in a quotation from Connick that the coloration of red glass was so dense that the piece would appear opaque if colored throughout, therefore only a thin layer of pigment was applied to an otherwise colorless piece. There is reason to doubt this, for it is possible to diffuse red pigment throughout the entire thickness of a piece of glass and still produce transparent red glass of varying degrees of brightness and saturation.[26] Without the microscopic laminations, however, one cannot simulate the glowing from within, the 'self-lighting' quality so commonly associated with the ruby in medieval times. In addition to this, there is another property in true gems which the glassworker might have tried to imitate in his laminated glass. This is called dichroism, or more properly, pleochroism, which refers to the ability of many genuine stones to exhibit a succession of different colors as they are turned in the hand. Glass, on the other hand, is singly refracting, and never dichroic, its index of refraction rarely exceeding 1.65, while that of genuine stones ranges up to 2.4.

A spectrophotometric analysis of Chartres fragments made at the Case Institute of Technology may provide a clue for a possible explanation of this lamination in the reds. The 'color curve' of blue glass showed a wider spread (a characteristic of cobalt), which included the red wavelengths in small proportion, while the red glass registered solely in the red area of the spectrum. The blue glass, therefore, tends to have more of the property of dichroism than the reds, with the subordinated red rays acting subtly on the receptors of the eye. The light rays from the red colorant, however, belong to a more restricted segment of the spectrum and are less dichroic. Increased vibrancy, however, is given to ruby glass by the multiple laminations which, by their constant flux and rearrangement, occasionally allow bright gleams or microscopic pencils of white light to shine through the color mass, giving the individual pieces a *vitesse* which makes them glow and vibrate like precious stones (see Fig. 9). While at a distance the spectator is not aware of these tiny bright spots, the glass seems to him to possess an extraordinary excitement, reminding him of jewels. The pencils of white light, of course, contain all the colors of the spectrum, and therefore make the red fragment to a certain degree pleochroic. This is a slender hypothesis, based on the slenderest evidence, but it is advanced as a suggestion for more thorough and extensive investigations.

In addition to the jewel-like fabrication of Chartres glass, certain devices commonly associated with goldsmithing appear frequently in the west windows of Chartres. The *Madonna and Child* panel from the central window (Fig. 1) illustrates the use of 'pearling' or 'beading' in the dotted white concentric borders enframing the principal figures, in the quadrant links at the four corners of the panel, and also in the triumphal-arch motif within the roundel. In goldsmithing, small beads or seed pearls were employed for similar areas; or, if jewels were not used, the metal was decorated by pouncing and repoussée work which produced a series of tiny, light-catching bosses projecting from the surface, enlivening the whole with its glittering effects. It is one of the oldest and commonest devices in metalwork, of any time or place, appearing especially when thinner metals like gold and silver are employed. It adds to the visual interest of the surface, enhancing the already lustrous material with glistening and twinkling accents. One of many examples is Figure 10, from the Carolingian altar in Milan Cathedral, in which the roundel is outlined by a similar concentric device composed of dotted accents.[27]

By the eighteenth century the process was reversed in certain respects, according to Didier d'Arclais de Montamy.[28] In a section entitled 'Memoire on artificial engraved stones,' the following passage occurs: 'The glass taken from old church windows is the best for making this type of cameo . . . it will take a beautiful polish, and does not scratch too easily . . .'[29] Montamy is also aware of the laminations within both stained glass and imitation gems.[30]

The intricate border surrounding the entire central window on the west façade of Chartres has been described as a foliate decoration with representations of birds and fantastic beasts. Instead, it could possibly be a splendid *collier,* a necklace joined by ruby links at regular intervals, and descending from the magnificent jeweled crown of the *Madonna in Glory* enthroned in the mandorla on the uppermost part of this window (see Fig. 4). Each segment contains bird or fantastic forms enframed by an interlacing of vines and foliage, reminiscent of a type of medieval necklace containing a series of stones upon which is engraved a variety of motifs inspired by the popular bestiaries, herbals, and lapidaries frequently serving as source books for the medieval artist. In its overall form the *collier* is derived from the art of heraldry, a possible source for many other elements and motifs in these windows, and an art also served extensively by the medieval jeweler and goldsmith.

CHAPTER IV

COLOR CHOICE AND COMPOSITION

In this chapter we will focus our attention on the color composition of several representative panels from the central window of the west façade. This splendid window describes the life of Christ in an ascending series of twenty-four panels, from the *Annunciation* to the *Entry into Jerusalem*, surmounted by six panels devoted to the *Glorification of the Madonna* in the uppermost part of the window. A rich border of foliate and animal decoration surrounds the entire ensemble, which was created about 1145–50.

With the exception of the *Glorification*, all of the panels are approximately square in physical dimension (1.02 meters wide and 1.05 meters high), and supported by iron armatures secured in the masonry at regular intervals and crossing at right angles. In the design of the glass, however, the square format is observed only in every other panel, alternating with roundel forms which frame the other scenes. This alternate system is also observed in the dominant color of each panel: blue background for the roundels and red for the squares, with fillet or 'beading' strips used in both types of enframement. We will concern ourselves with color choice and composition in four of these panels: two square and two round, employing red and blue grounds as described above.

All the panels, of course, have been repaired and restored from time to time, some more than others. It is as much a part of the aging process of a stained glass window to acquire new pieces of glass, additional painting and leading, as it is for old bronze to take on a characteristic patina. Exposed to extreme weather and temperature changes, these windows suffered constant damage even before the hand of man was able to make its alterations. This is especially true in the faces of the figures and in the pattern of the leads as they join the individual pieces of glass. Whenever a fracture occurs, for example, a strip of lead is inserted in the break, and in the case of more severe damage the configuration of the leading must follow the contour of the pieces of glass used as replacements. Therefore this

67

particular study will ignore, for the most part, the design of the lead strips as they subdivide the main color areas. We will deal with colors *en bloc*, for we have very little notion of the lead patterns as they originally appeared in our twelfth-century panels. We shall also ignore the horizontal saddle bars trisecting each window; they, too are modern. In earlier times it was customary to use more of them per window, often set at irregular angles, and sometimes made of wood.

The four scenes chosen for our discussion are *The Nativity*, *The Massacre of the Innocents*, *The Three Magi*, and *The Annunciation to the Shepherds*—two square and two round compositions with red and blue backgrounds, respectively, but differing within each type in mode of presentation, for two of the scenes, the *Annunciation to the Shepherds* and the *Massacre*, are episodic and dramatic in character, while the *Nativity* and *Three Magi* panels are more emblematic and formal in presentation.[1] As we proceed with our analyses of the colours in these panels it will become apparent that their skillful handling contributes as much to the various modes of presentation as do the other elements in the composition.

The *Nativity* scene (Fig. 11) contains very little to remind the spectator of the humble manger, except for the conventional heads of the ox and ass close to the newborn Christ. The Virgin, far from having the appearance of a simple peasant girl, is a regal, imposing figure, the Queen of Heaven reclining on a beautifully wrought golden bed as she raises her hand in majestic benediction. The entire scene is formal and sacerdotal in character, with the curtains of the sanctuary drawn back to reveal an important episode in the sacred drama. As Professor Karl Young has demonstrated, the twelfth century saw an extensive development of the liturgical drama, especially in connection with the Christmas and Easter festivals, and it is in the central, or *Christmas*, window of Chartres that many of these religious dramas are re-enacted.[2] Reinforcing the liturgical and ceremonial nature of the scene is the lamp hanging above the heads of the figures and the altar supporting the Christ Child, the *Corpus Verum*.[3] The altar is a characteristic four-columned type used in France and the Mosan region during this period.

1. *Madonna and Child*. Central Window, West Façade. Twelfth century

2. *The Annunciation.* Central Window, West Façade. Twelfth century

3. *The Presentation in the Temple*. Central Window, West Façade. Twelfth century

4. *The Glorification of the Virgin*. Central Window, West Façade. Twelfth century

5. *La Belle Verrière*. South Ambulatory. Twelfth century

6. Microphotograph: 5 mm. edge of modern 'lined' red glass

7. Microphotograph: 3 mm. edge of Chartres twelfth-century 'flashed' red glass

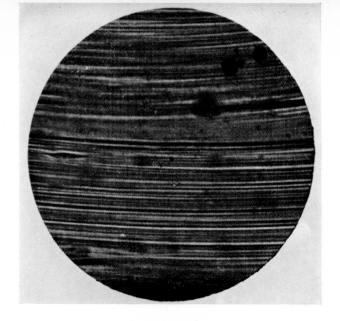

8. Microphotograph of artificial ruby (from Escard, *Les pierres précieuses*. Plate XXIII, fig. 4)

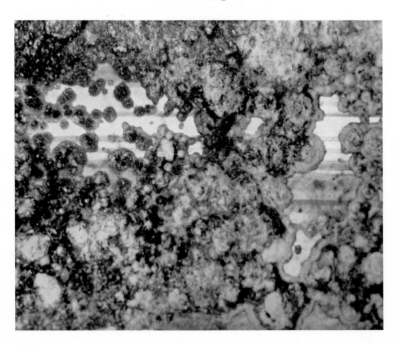

9. Microphotograph of weathered side of Chartres thirteenth-century red glass, showing coating and light streaks

10. *A Scene from the Life of St. Ambrose.* Gold relief on altar frontal.
S. Ambrogio, Milan. Ninth century

11. *The Nativity.* Central Window, West Façade. Twelfth century

12. *The Massacre of the Innocents*. Central Window, West Façade. Twelfth century

13. *The Three Magi*. Central Window, West Façade. Twelfth century

14. *The Annunciation to the Shepherds*. Central Window, West Façade. Twelfth century

The color scheme of this window is quite simple—based on three colors: red, blue, and gold—as well as white, with very small areas of green and lemon-yellow below the golden bed of the Virgin. There is also a thin extension of green above and behind the Virgin representing the cushions on the bed, but in the reproduction this area appears as blue or greenish-blue. The figure of Joseph has been so unskillfully restored that I do not wish to include either him or his garments in this discussion, and the same may be said for the face of the Virgin, as both are the work of the nineteenth century.

Red as the background color in this scene reinforces the sense of enclosure and limited spatial depth. The color seems to advance toward us, enveloping and binding together all elements of the composition on a somewhat unified plane. The curtains, for example, seem to be sustained as much by the surrounding color as by rods and stays, and all the compositional units are in a sense immobilized and frozen in a solid structural unity by this coalescing medium.

It is more than a coincidence, I believe, that red is used as a background color for panels in the central window depicting events in enclosed areas, e.g., the *Annunciation, Nativity, King Herod, Presentation in the Temple, Fall of the Egyptian Idols*, and the *Dream of Joseph* (to cite the most important), while scenes taking place outdoors or in celestial settings are seen against blue, as in the *Visitation, Annunciation to the Shepherds, Dream of the Magi, Flight to Egypt*, the *Baptism*, and the *Glorification of the Madonna*. Three panels are devoted to the *Massacre of the Innocents* (the *Ordo Rachelis*), beginning with King Herod commanding his soldiers—an interior scene—followed by two panels showing the massacre, one a roundel against blue and the other balancing the Herod panel in its square and red format. Exceptions to this tendency are the *Entry into Jerusalem* (against red) and the angels flanking the *Glorification of the Madonna*.

Continuing with the red background of the *Nativity*, and following its outline from the top of the composition near the lamp and down along the lower edges of the curtains, we find that it forms a sort of canopy or baldachin over the Holy Family, with the Christ Child in the center, descending in a thin strip to

F

envelop the Vigin more completely than Joseph on the right. The Christ Child is wholly enclosed within this area except for a small area touching the halos of his parents. The red area is adjusted to perfect equilibrium by balancing the thin vertical strip on the left with the large bloc between Joseph and the altar.

A remarkable symmetry and order is achieved within this composition. The quiet and stable appearance is attained in large part by the use of blue in repeated horizontal shapes and broad, unbroken areas, first in the Christ Child (strictly parallel to the lower frame), the reclining form of the Virgin and the blue stripes of the curtains. The golden altar also serves as an anchor of stability in its absolute centrality and regularity, while the slightly diagonal position of the golden bed of Mary with its larger head portion is offset in occult balance by the prominent golden star on the upper right, which also echoes the halo of the Virgin. The quiet composure and stability of this scene is established as much by the choice and composition of colors as by compositional devices, with the cool tones of *bleu du ciel* and white counterbalancing the powerful reds, while the gold serves as an intermediary between the extremes, as it does in the spectrum. Moreover, the points of contact between the colors are smooth and flowing, avoiding jagged or irregular penetrations of one positive color into another. The lines between the blues and reds flow gently in graceful curves, and the only areas of sharp penetration into the red are colorless, that is, the heads of the animals, the censer, and the upraised arm of the Virgin, giving one a sense of relief when seen against the dense reds, rather than an impression of agitation. This scene, with its balance and order and restraint, is quite classical in character. Additional structural stability is achieved by the repeated verticals of gold in the bed posts and altar columns. In pure design, this composition achieves a perfect balance in its horizontal and vertical components.

A dramatic contrast to the formality and composure of the *Nativity* is provided by the turbulent *Massacre of the Innocents* (Fig. 12), composed also within a square format and against a red ground, but treated in such a manner that it conveys the extreme agitation and torment of the episode. While the dominant colors are the same—red, blue and gold—they are spotted and juxtaposed in effective and moving patterns which set up conflicts and tensions throughout.

The design itself contains many elements breaking out beyond its frame: the sharp sword of the soldier on the left, his right heel, the hand of the murdered infant, the foot of the wailing mother, and the head and hand of another victim on the right. In its colors, the blues are deeper and stronger than the celestial blues of the *Nativity* (although in the color plates they appear quite the same), and the golds incline toward the tawny, becoming brownish toward the right. There is much less white used in this panel, and where it appears it is not in broad, regular areas, but placed in thin strips or smaller units in eccentric spotting.

Broken in continuity by heads, swords and other elements pointing out in many directions, the red ground in the *Massacre* does not flow gracefully from side to side, unifying the composition. Rather, it is separated in blocks resting uneasily on points placed off-center or on irregular projections into other colors. In the lower half, there is a quick, scattered spotting of reds, adding sharp staccato accents to an area already charged with action.

At first the blue seems to be a stabilizing factor, setting up a strong vertical axis in the garments of the central mother and the nearby soldier, but other blue areas like the skirt of the woman below, or the legs of the soldier on the left, veer from the axis just enough to add a strained and discordant element, not sufficiently to establish a positive countermotion or direction, but in the way that a musical instrument sometimes has a string going out of tune not a complete interval but enough to make it 'edgy'—as musicians say—when it is sounded along with other notes. Especially painful is the angle of the lower part of the sword on the right, while the other weapon in the upraised hand of the left soldier stabs through the deep red ground and even breaks through the frame in the fury of its motion. The rhythm of the blues is chaotic when we compare this agitated panel to the *Nativity*, where the rhythmic pattern is simple and easily discernible, a one-two-three, one-two sequence from top to bottom. It is doubtful that any two people would agree on a rhythmic pattern for the colors of the confused and turbulent *Massacre*, for there appears to be a purposeful discoordination and confusion in the arrangement of its color and design.

As abstract shapes, the blue areas frequently have unlovely projections and off-balance forms, as in the upper garments of the soldiers, which in their several borders come in contact with various colors: red, yellow, gold, and brown. Moreover, there are prominent areas in this panel in which a strong green is used, juxtaposed directly with blue: the *bottes* of the left soldier (actually very green in the panel), whose color scheme is reversed on the legs of the child he is about to slay, and the outer garment of the kneeling woman which cuts sharply and discordantly between two blue areas. A spot of green also appears on the sleeve of the same soldier, just below the sword he holds aloft. The golds are also scattered about in irregular shapes and rhythms, adding to the general sense of imbalance and chaos.

Considering the use of red in these two panels—a color which, when heavily saturated and intense, is usually associated with activity, aggression, and excitement—one marvels that a totally different effect has been achieved in these two compositions when the same fiery background is employed. It is probably brought under control in the *Nativity* by the reposeful shapes in which it is cast, and it is also counterbalanced by cool tones of blue and white, as part of a very simple color scheme. The *Massacre*, on the other hand, contains very few cool or neutral colors to offset the intensity of the reds. Instead, the warm blues, golds, and greens, juxtaposed directly with the reds without any relieving areas, add further to the turbulence and excitement of the visual field.

For a decided change of mood and tempo let us turn to one of the roundel panels, the sumptuous and majestic *Three Magi* (Fig. 13), with their golden crowns and multicolored robes.[4] In oriental splendor the Three Kings stand in court audience before King Herod, who sits enthroned in an adjacent panel (not shown). Their costumes are magnificent—of the most costly materials—and even sewn with pearls and bands of precious stones—with colors ranging from rich browns to moss-green and sea-green, bright yellows and crimsons, purples, and magentas. The uncomplicated blue background is a perfect foil for the richness and elaboration of the foreground figures. It is exceedingly stable, serving as a counteraction to the turning movements of the Kings, and almost architectural as it extends slender, regularly spaced 'columns' between the three figures, serving also to separate them, avoiding overlapping and tension.

The blues, being more receding in color effect than the reds, have a tendency to allow the figures to stand out from the ground to a greater degree, yet they are in no sense presented as plastic or three-dimensional forms. They seem, however, slightly more detached and 'floating' than figures seen against a red ground. This, however, presents the artist with certain problems, for in an atmosphere of blue within a circle there is great danger that the figures will lose their bearings and have a tendency to gyrate or move about within the smooth, curved contour. This is prevented in the *Three Magi* panel through several devices: first, by the strong vertical axes of the Kings, reinforced by the upright staffs in their hands. Furthermore, the staffs of the two outside Kings impinge on the circle both top and bottom, as if to pin it down and stabilize it, with the en-encircling frame a strong red, giving it an appearance of solidity in contrast to the less assertive quality of the blue. The two outer Kings also turn toward the outside, their movements counteracting the concavity of the circle, while their feet establish footholds by penetrating into the frame. Moreover, the small counter-circles upon which two of the kings stand are additional stabilizing elements, as well as a clever device to keep them on the same level as the central King.

Choice of color adds to the sense of balance and stability in the *Three Magi* panel. The central axis is established by the deeper and richer reds, magentas and purples of the central King, and flanking him are figures dressed in colors of less 'heavy' appearance—light greens, bright yellows, with passages of white here and there, along with simulated jewels. The outside figures counterbalance each other in the use of green, on one for the outer cloak and on the other for the inner garment. Something of a triangular scheme is established between the magenta-colored hems on the lower robes of the outside Kings and the inner vestment and sleeve of the central figure.

Representations of tiny rows of precious stones sewn on the Kings' robes add bright overtones to the already rich color chords presented by these figures. Emeralds, rubies, pearls, topazes, and amethysts appear in rows along hems of robes and in diagonal bands on outer garments. They seem to provide a directional emphasis, leading the eye from the King on the left to the middle King where the lines diverge and then to the right figure which carries the eye in an upward diagonal direction. Our eyes are then turned back to the red staff on the right, and also arrested by the powerful reverse twist of the third King, whose head and upper torso turn in a counter-direction to his feet and legs. A more positive color—red—is used for the staff on the right, while white, which does not seem to be as much of a barrier to communication or transition, is used on the left, in the direction of the adjoining panel, which depicts King Herod, with whom the Three Kings are conversing.

From *le style courtois* of the *Three Magi* we turn now to a genre episode in the *Annunciation to the Shepherds* (Fig. 14). Immediately we notice that this is the only scene in the entire window with an imperfect enframement, for the roundel is irregular—as if drawn freehand—in contrast to the perfect circles and squares of the other panels. Was this a mistake, done by a careless or unskilled assistant? The work inside the frame shows no lack of competence, for the scene has great charm and freshness, with the shepherds and angels in lively attitudes. I suspect that this imperfection—or better, irregularity—was intentional, related perhaps to certain formulas and devices in the art of heraldry which were gaining wide acceptance during the twelfth century. Many of the earliest heraldic devices taken up by noble families were based on the square and the circle in various combinations, appearing on shields as *échiquier*, *annelets d'argent*, *besans* and *tourteaux*, comparatively simple designs associated with families of the most ancient lineage, and for this reason often given the heraldic classification of *pièces honorables*.[5] Most of the panels of this central window (located directly above the sculptured *Royal*

Portal with its kings and queens of Judah—and of France) are
concerned with regal or celestial figures, and the entire format
—including style, color, and costume—is courtly, rich and
aristocratic, with the exception of the shepherds' scene which is
genre and rustic in character. Could this account for the irregular enframement used for this episode? It represents a variation from the formal and courtly mode of presentation, which
in less emblematic types of art is achieved in other ways, as in
the *Portinari Altarpiece*, for example, where the shepherds are
homely peasant figures, rough-textured, while the Virgin and
angels are graceful and idealized forms.

Within this irregular frame, the blue background is the same
rich, intense blue we have seen in the rest of the window in
the other roundel panels, thereby achieving a pervasive, unifying tonality. A decided color change is found in the *Annunciation to the Shepherds*, however, where we see new tones in the
costumes of the shepherds not encountered in any other panel
of the central window. There is a slight admixture of brownish
coloring in the gold and mauve of their costumes, causing
especially in the latter a raisin-like tonality particularly in the
darker portions, suggesting homespun and coarser materials.
This, combined with the liveliness and spontaneity of their
gestures, establishes an entirely different mode from the aristocratic and formal presentation of the other panels, much in the
same way that shepherds' songs probably differed in tonal and
rhythmic modalities from the more courtly lyrics of the period.
A similar distinction in treatment and interpretation is seen in
the sculpture of the *Royal Portal* where the delightful shepherd
group over the right doorway provides a charming contrast to
the solemn figures below. This group has a way of suggesting
the simple tones of a shepherd's pipe.

In the *Annunciation to the Shepherds*, the clothes of these
figures (with the possible exception of the shepherd on the left)
cannot be associated in stained glass terminology with the
names of precious stones, which is certainly the case with the
splendid costumes of the regal and celestial personages in the
other panels, where richly colored glass simulating ruby, topaz,
emerald, and sapphire is extensively employed. The popular
lapidaries of the twelfth century (especially the famous

Lapidaire of Bishop Marbode, translated many times into the vernacular) are full of references to jewels in their association with divinity, kingship and nobility, as well as the usual miraculous and supernatural powers ascribed to these stones. But this association is found less in the colors of the shepherds, where a suggestion of earth tones prevails. On the other hand, the colors used for the nobles appear to be more heraldic in nature.

Contributing to the animation of this scene, the blue background is rendered in lively zigzag patterns between the figures, accenting and dramatizing the upward flow of excitement and wonder from the shepherds and, in the opposite direction, the divine energy and flying motions of the angels. The blue area between the two angels on the right suggests a Baroque spiral twist, being full of energetic pulsations and counterdirections, and a further sense of restlessness is achieved by basing the blue areas on pointed or off-center foundations, with their upper segments also pointed.

Something of a chiasmic pattern is seen in the echoing gestures of the angels and shepherds, as well as in the diagonal spotting of colors—the golds of the left shepherd and the right angel, and the varied mauves or violets of the other angel and shepherds. Another diagonal is set up by the dog on the lower right and the white tunic of the angel above. Stability is achieved by the vertical axis of the central shepherd, his bright red leggings, and the triangular outline created by the gold of the shepherd, the angel above, and the tree trunk on the lower right. This is reinforced by the directions in which the shepherds are facing, their counter-gestures, staffs and attitudes. On the brightness scale, moreover, a balance is struck, for the two figures in dull mauve are offset by the shepherd in bright gold, with an even brighter gold reserved for the angel on high.

The panels we have examined are united in several ways. We have observed in all of them a correspondence between the choice and arrangement of colors and the expressive meaning of the story. Appropriate modalities and compositions of color have been chosen to fit episodes of widely varying character, with one incident intensified by exciting color shapes and juxtapositions and another given an arresting solemnity by judicious tonal control and balance. As a general principle it could be stated that there is a close connection in this art between color scheme and composition and the implicit meaning and expression of various scenes. According to my observations, this principle may also be applied to other panels of this twelfth-century window which in the same manner employ color as luminous and expressive form. The glass designers of this period—with all their daring use of light and color—were not abstract painters, for they were interested in a particular content to be expressed, and they adapted their means to it from panel to panel, while at the same time sustaining the total harmony of the window through the use of certain color constants—principally red and blue—repeated throughout the ensemble as alternate ground colors and counterbalancing hues. This repetitive use of color is another device employed by the artist to unite all the component panels within the total harmony of the window. A blue roundel is surrounded by a red frame, and a solid red ground is offset by figures richly dressed in blue, while in other panels the reverse is seen. As we have noted earlier, the scenes in the central window are presented within alternate red squares and blue circles in strict and unvarying succession, thereby requiring of the artist a careful discipline and no little ingenuity in creating a wide range of episodes within this simple and somewhat restrictive formula. Yet through skillful use of color the twelfth-century glassmaker was able to achieve a variety of modes and tempos within this emblematic art, combining visual éclat and symbolical form with extraordinary effectiveness.

Other distinctive features of this art become apparent in the light of subsequent developments in stained glass, when toward the end of the Gothic period the element of color is used for other ends, chiefly, the imitation of nature and the suggestion of spatial depth. Fourteenth- and fifteenth-century glass often displayed richly colored figures against light backgrounds, giving them a three-dimensional and freestanding appearance in clear space, frequently reinforcing this impression by architectural canopies over their heads—a direct reference to current spatial attitudes in sculpture. Figure and ground no longer cohere, and for the first time we can speak of background in the conventional sense. The surrounding color is no longer used to organize on one plane, to coalesce and unify in a 'homogeneous fabric of light' (as Panofsky so felicitously describes it), but rather to set off some of the foreground elements. With the Renaissance we come to the full development in this direction, for here color is employed to simulate the appearance of nature—including atmospheric space—and in this period we have the curious experience of seeing 'through a window' in a window . . . an idea never occurring to the artists of the twelfth century.

The colors in our windows appear in equal strength for both figures and ground, with neither area subordinate to the other. Moreover, these powerful and absolute colors are interchangeable, used alternately in figure and ground to suggest a 'consubstantiality' of luminous form in which all elements exist in a new order of being. The close integration of figure and surrounding area—seen also in Romanesque sculpture—begins to break down towards the end of the twelfth century, and with the onset of the fully developed Gothic style the visual field tends to separate itself into more distinct planes. Foreshadowings of this tendency are apparent in the panels of the *Passion* window, which in my opinion is not coeval with the adjoining central and *Jesse* windows but probably dates much later in the century, for here the foreground and narrative elements receive increasing emphasis, upsetting the traditional balance by occupying a greater proportion of the total field in many instances while the ground color is reduced in area and importance.

The thirteenth century added new complexities through inventive elaboration in the shape and design of panels and the increased emphasis on picturesque motifs of foliage, architecture, and other elements against the background. At the same time, in other panels, we encounter frequent returns to the more formal principles of the twelfth century in which the colors of figure and background are allowed once again to play an equally positive role, for this was an art not easily forgotten, especially when produced under the spell of these windows in the same Cathedral. A subtle change takes place, however, in the expressive language of the design, for in the later art the figures become more and more the vehicles of dramatic and narrative expression at the expense of the surrounding field, while in the Romanesque panels a condition of equilibrium is maintained, with all component elements contributing, according to their capacity, to a new and expressive unity in light and color.

NOTES

NOTES TO CHAPTER ONE

1. Louis Grodecki, in his studies of windows in the Cathedral of Auxerre, Saint-Urbain of Troyes, and Sainte-Radegonde of Poitiers, has noted that figures in deep colors lose their power when set against light grounds of grisaille. 'Le vitrail et l'architecture au XIIᵉ et au XIIIᵉ siècles,' *Gazette des Beaux-Arts*, II, 1949, pp. 17–18. The nineteenth-century French scientist and color authority, Michel Chevreul, observed in the nave of Nôtre Dame in Paris the unfortunate juxtaposition of light and dark windows: '... the effect of the latter is diminished by the former when their rays arrive at the eye at the same time.' *Comptes rendus*, LVII, Paris, 1863, p. 662.

2. LeGrand Hardy, 'The Eye as Affected by Illumination,' *Transactions of the Illuminating Engineering Society*, XXIX, 1934, p. 381. In this article, Hardy calls for 'a more intelligent cooperation between the illuminating engineer, the architect and the ophthalmologist who have up to the present never adequately been en rapport' (p. 382). See also Hamilton Hartridge, *Recent Advances in the Physiology of Vision*, London, 1950, p. 216; W. D. Wright, *The Perception of Light*, London, 1938, pp. 36–61; J. H. Parsons, *An Introduction to the Study of Colour Vision*, Cambridge, England, 1924, passim.

3. G. Bontemps, *Peinture sur verre*, Paris, 1845, p. 40. See also the same author's *Guide du verrier*, Paris, 1868, passim.

4. W. Sturrock and K. A. Staley, *Fundamentals of Light and Lighting*, Cleveland, General Electric Corporation, 1953, p. 35.

5. Wright (*op. cit.*, p. 61) asserts that glare is greater the more intense the glare source, and the lower the intensity of the major area, for the latter produces a lower adaptation level and a higher contrast.

6. H. Hartridge, *op. cit.*, p. 216.

7. H. von Helmholtz, *Physiological Optics*, tr. Southall, New York, 1924, I, p. 319, Fig. 60.

8. Henri Focillon, *Art d'occident*, Paris, 1947, p. 248.

9. Louis Grodecki, 'Le vitrail et l'architecture au XIIᵉ et au XIIIᵉ siècles,' (*op. cit.*), p. 11.

10. J. E. Purkinje, *Beobachtungen und Versuche zur Physiologie der Sinne*, II, Berlin, 1825, p. 110. Purkinje also published *Beiträge zur Kenntnis des Sehens in subjektiver Hinsicht*, Prague, 1819; and *Neue Beiträge etc.*, Berlin, 1825. There is an extensive literature on the Purkinje phenomenon and twilight vision. See esp. Helmholtz, *op. cit.*, II, Appendix by W. Nagel, 'Adaptation, Twilight Vision, and the Duplicity Theory,' pp. 313–394; Ragnar Granit, *Sensory Mechanisms of the Retina*, London, 1947, pp. 258–259, and Fig. 125; John W. T. Walsh, *Photometry*, London, 1953, pp. 73–74, Fig. 44; W. D. Wright, *The Measurement of Colour*, London, 1944, pp. 1–33; George Wald and Donald R. Griffin, 'The Change in Refractive Power of the Human Eye in Dim and Bright Light,' in *Journal of the Optical Society of America*, XXXVII, 1947, pp. 321–336.

11. *De Coloribus*, 792 a.

12. J. A. S. Kinney, 'Sensitivity of the Eye to Spectral Radiation at Scotopic and Mesopic Intensity Level,' in *Journal of the Optical Society of America*, July, 1955, pp. 507–514.

13. *Ibid.* See also Yun Hsia and C. Graham, 'Spectral Sensitivity of the Cones in the Dark Adapted Human Eye,' *Proceedings of the National Academy of Sciences,* XXXVIII, 1952, pp. 80–85.

14. G. Wald and D. R. Griffin, 'The Change in Refractice Power of the Human Eye in Dim and Bright Light,' *Journal of the Optical Society of America,* XXXVII, 1947, 321–336.

15. C. E. Ferree and G. Rand, 'The Effect of Variation of Visual Angle, Intensity, and Composition of Light on Important Ocular Functions,' *Transactions of the Illuminating Engineering Society,* XVII, 1922, pp. 69–102.

16. David Katz, *The World of Colour,* London, 1935, p. 179.

17. Translated by Erwin Panofsky, *Abbot Suger on the Abbey Church of Saint-Denis,* Princeton, 1946, p. 65.

NOTES TO CHAPTER TWO

1. Paul Gout, *Viollet-le-Duc, sa vie, son œuvre, sa doctrine,* Paris, Champion, 1914, p. 33.

2. *Ibid.*

3. *Ibid.,* p. 38.

4. Viollet-le-Duc, E., 'Vitrail,' in *Dictionnaire raisonné de l'architecture française* (9 vols.), Paris, 1854–1868, IX, pp. 373–462. Hereafter cited as *Vitrail.*

5. Marcel Aubert, *Vitraux des églises de France,* Paris, Éditions du Chêne, 1947, p. 29.

6. Louis Grodecki, *Vitraux de France,* Paris, 1953, p. 23.

7. *Congrès archéologique de France,* XCVII, 1934, p. 293.

8. Marcel Aubert, *Le Vitrail en France,* Paris, 1946, p. 13.

9. Charles J. Connick, *Adventures in Light and Color,* New York, 1937. See especially p. 20, and Plate V.

10. R. Sowers, *The Lost Art, A Survey of One Thousand Years of Stained Glass,* New York, 1954, p. 33. Similar sentiments are expressed in the chief organ of the stained glass profession in America, *Stained Glass.* In the winter 1946 issue, Henry Lee Willet declared that 'Vitrail is the basis of all stained glass teaching' (p. 108). For a more recent opinion by Mr. Sowers, see *The Art Bulletin,* XLV, 4, December 1963, p. 399.

11. *Vitrail,* p. 390.

12. *Ibid.,* pp. 379–380.

13. Ellen Simon of Toronto and New York.

14. It is possible that the design of the experimental panel was suggested to Viollet-le-Duc by the arrangement of the panels in the central window of Chartres' west façade, which consists basically of alternate red squares and blue roundels.

15. Viollet-le-Duc gives no specifications for light sources in this experiment. My own observations were made under various daylight conditions: morning and afternoon, bright and overcast, with and without direct sunlight on the panel.

16. *Vitrail,* p. 398.

17. During the twelfth and thirteenth centuries a great variety of 'white' glass was employed, never completely colorless in appearance because

of traces of certain metallic oxides which produced a wide range of tints, especially light green and pink. This glass, moreover, was usually coated with grisaille.

18. *Vitrail,* pp. 383–384.

19. *Ibid.,* pp. 421–422.

20. Perhaps the worst example of modern overpainting is the *Head of Christ* from Wissembourg, now in the Museum at Strasbourg. Some of the glass possibly dates from the eleventh century, but the features are a hideous modern caricature of Romanesque style. *Cf.* Marcel Aubert *et al., Le vitrail français,* Paris, 1958, p. 73.

21. A contemporary of Viollet-le-Duc, Lucien Magne, made different observations in the Cathedral of Châlons-sur-Marne. *L'Œuvre des peintres verriers français,* Paris, 1885, p. xi.

22. Heinrich Oidtmann, *Die Glasmalerei,* Cologne, Vol. I, 1893; Vol. II, 1898.

23. *Ibid.,* II, 152. N. Westlake also disagrees with this point. *A History of Design on Painted Glass,* London, 1881, I, pp. 61–62.

24. *Ibid.,* II, p. 126.

25. *Ibid.,* pp. 127–128.

26. *Vitrail,* p. 387. Subsequent writers to our own time have repeated this erroneous observation.

27. Cobalt was the chief colorant for this glass, with the addition of manganese oxide to deepen the color. *Cf.* G. Chesneau, 'Contribution à l'étude chimique des vitraux du moyen-âge,' *Comptes rendus, Académie des Sciences,* Paris, CLX, 1915, pp. 286–287. By a spectrophotometric analysis of Chartres fragments in my possession, Professor Earnest Jaeger of the Chemistry Department, Western Reserve University, has also found manganese and cobalt in this glass.

28. Chesneau *(Ibid.,* p. 286) calls this the cobalt blue, without the deepening addition of manganese oxide.

29. Plateau, 'Mémoire sur l'irradiation,' *Nouveaux mémoires de l'Académie Royale, Brussels,* XI, 1838, pp. 1–113. Also 'Sur l'irradiation,' *Bulletin, Académie des Sciences,* Brussels, IV, 1837, pp. 355–358; and VI, 1839, pp. 501–505. A summary of his findings was published in Paris in 1839, *Comptes rendus,* VIII, pp. 883–886. Plateau was Professor of Physics and Astronomy at the University of Ghent, and from 1852 to his death in 1883, he was Correspondent to the Académie des Sciences in Paris.

30. Galileo, Galilei, *Opere,* Bologna, Dozza, 1656, pp. 103–123: 'Lettera del Sig. Galileo Galilei al Padre Christoforo Grienberger della Compagnia di Giesù, in materia della Montuosità della Luna.'

31. Plateau, 'Mémoire sur l'irradiation,' *op. cit.,* p. 111.

32. *Ibid.* 'Descartes est, je pense, le premier qui ait expliqué l'irradiation par une propagation de l'impression sur la rétine.' *Cf.* Descartes, *La dioptrique,* Leyden, 1637, discours sixième, pp. 67 et 68.

33. Helmholtz, *op. cit.,* II, pp. 186–188. The German scientist takes exception, however, to Plateau's explanation for the cause of irradiation, the *synaesthesia* or sympathetic sensations of adjacent retinal fibres. 'Today we know that this is not the true reason. . . . Actually, the rays do not converge exactly on one point on the retina, but on an area around this point, that one called the circle of diffusion. Every bright spot has a circle of diffusion, therefore they overflow their geometric contours at the expense of the surrounding dark area.' See also E. Brücke, *Bruch-*

stücke aus der Theorie der Bildenden Künste, Leipzig, Brockhaus, 1877, translated into the French *Principes scientifiques des beaux-arts*, Paris, Baillière, 1878, p. 137. Twentieth-century scientists suggest that irregular refractions of light in the eye are a partial explanation for the phenomenon of irradiation, but are still in disagreement over retinal processes and physiological causes. W. D. Wright points out that in the cone-dominant foveal area of the retina each cone is connected to only one nerve fibre, while in the rod-dominated periphery as many as sixty to one hundred rods are sometimes found to converge on a common fibre. *The Perception of Light*, London, 1938, p. 4. When the eye is accommodated to a dark interior, as in a cathedral, there occurs a partial Purkinje shift, with increased activity in the area of the rods and a heightened impression of irradiation. See also E. N. Willmer, *Retinal Structure and Colour Vision*, Cambridge, England, 1946, pp. 3–20.

34. Helmholtz, *op. cit.*, I, pp. 172–203.
35. Lewis F. Day, *Windows, A Book about Stained and Painted Glass*, London, 1902, p. 34.
36. *Ibid.*, p. 35.
37. Brücke, *Die Physiologie der Farben*, Leipzig, Braumüller, 1866, published in French with the title *Des couleurs*, (tr. J. Schutzenberger), Paris, Baillière, 1866.
38. Brücke, *op cit.*, Ger. ed., p. 181; Fr. ed., p. 212.
39. *Ibid.*, Ger. ed., p. 165; Fr. ed., p. 194.
40. *Ibid.*, Ger. ed., p. 180; Fr. ed., p. 211.
41. Ernst Brücke, *Bruchstücke aus der Theorie der bildenden Künste*, Leipzig, 1877.
42. Ernst Brücke and H. von Helmholtz, *Principes scientifiques des beaux-arts*, Paris, Baillière, 1866.
43. M. E. Chevreul, *De la loi du contraste simultané des couleurs*, Paris, Pitois-Levrault, 1839, 2 vols.
44. 'Mémoire sur les vitraux peints,' *Comptes rendus*, Académie des Sciences, Paris, LVII, 1863, pp. 655–666.
45. According to Proposition 5 of the 1839 edition on *Simultaneous Contrast*, the juxtaposition of blue and red would see the blue inclining to green and the red to yellow. 'The modifications of contiguous colors are precisely such as would result from the addition to each of them of the color which is complementary to its neighbor.' (Prop. 17.)
46. M. E. Chevreul, *op. cit.*, section 438. 'They produce all their effect only when they present the strongest harmonies of contrast ... intense colors of red, blue, orange, violet and yellow.' (*Idem.*) Chevreul's observations on stained glass are contained in sections 430–438.
47. *Viollet-le-Duc, ses travaux d'art et son système archéologique*, Paris, L'Année Archéologique, 1881, p. 43.
48. *Ibid.*, p. 42.
49. *Ibid.* In another source, Viollet-le-Duc says: 'Il ne faut avoir trop raison en ce monde...' *Pages inédites*, quoted in Paul Gout, *Viollet-le-Duc*, Paris, 1914, p. xi.
50. George Field, *Chromatics, or An Essay on the Analogy and Harmony of Colors*, London, Newman, 1817, pp. 1–32.
51. George Field, *Chromatics*, London, 1858 ed., p. 6. This edition was also entitled: *Rudiments of the Painters' Art, or A Grammar of Colouring*.

G

52. George Field, *Chromatics,* London, 1856.

53. *Art Journal,* London, XIII (New Series), 1874, p. 211.

54. *Ibid.*

55. *The Fine Arts Courts in the Crystal Palace,* London, Bradbury and Evans, 1854, p. 34. This is a later reprint of the guidebook, the original having come out in 1851. (In 1853, a similar declaration appeared in connection with New York City's Crystal Palace, with Henry Greenough, brother of the sculptor Horatio, using the same words, probably taken from an earlier guidebook of Jones. *Putnam's Monthly,* II, August 1853, p. 125. Horace Greeley describes this structure as 'Moorish architecture with Byzantine decoration.') Jones established his reputation as a decorator and color authority upon the publication in 1842 of the sumptuous volume, *The Alhambra* (London), which was sponsored by a distinguished list of personages headed by the rulers of England and France. The text was in English and French, and some of the drawings were done by a French artist, Jules Goury, an early collaborator with Jones, but who unfortunately died while the book was in preparation. The section on the Alhambra in the guidebook is an abridgement of the 1842 text.

56. Jones, *The Fine Arts Courts,* etc., p. 45.

57. *The Builder,* VIII, pp. 604, 613.

58. Jones, *The Grammar of Ornament,* London, 1856, p. 5.

59. *Vitrail,* p. 395. *Cf. The Alhambra,* I, text for Plate 38.

60. As evidence of the prestige enjoyed by Viollet-le-Duc in England, a quotation from his *Dictionnaire de mobilier français* is used on the title page of Charles Eastlake's *Hints on Household Taste* (2nd ed., London, 1869). A personal encounter between Jones and Viollet-le-Duc was not unlikely. Jones went to France on several occasions, and one of his most important trips involved a mission to borrow works of art from the French government for the London exhibition of 1850.

61. Brücke, *Die Physiologie der Farben, loc. cit.,* p. 294.

62. John Wilkinson, *On Colour,* London, 1858. See especially pp. xii–xiii.

63. *Ibid.,* pp. 42–53.

64. *Ibid.,* p. 47. *Cf. Vitrail,* pp. 421–422.

65. A clear distinction between these explanations is given in R. B. Braithewaite, *Scientific Explanation,* Cambridge, England 1955, pp. 320–333. See also E. Nagel, 'Pure Science and Gross Experience,' *New Republic,* CXXI, 1949, pp. 20–23. I wish to thank Professor Meyer Schapiro for these references.

66. M. R. Almack, 'A Quantitative Study of Chromatic Adaptation,' *Psychological Monographs,* XXXVIII, 2, 1928, p. 25.

67. For the essential differences between additive and subtractive color mixtures, see *The Science of Color,* ed. Committee on Colorimetry, New York, Optical Society of America, 1953, pp. 38–40. See also W. D. Wright, *The Measurement of Colour,* London, 1944, p. 48: 'When the red, green and blue lights are mixed in certain proportions they produce white; when any one of the three is predominant, the result will be a desaturated red, green, or blue as the case may be, while if any two of the three are predominant, the colour will be a desaturated yellow, blue-green, or purple.'

NOTES TO CHAPTER THREE

1. Pliny, *Natural History*, XXXVI, 67.
2. For these microphotographs I am indebted to the patience and skill of Dr. Hugh McCorkle and Dr. Edgar Bowerfind of the Institute of Pathology, Western Reserve University.
3. The term 'flashed glass' is often used to describe many types of coated glass, but here it will be applied only to those examples produced by the traditional methods of the twelfth and thirteenth centuries in which the coating is acquired or 'gathered' before the blowing, a method resulting in a subtly fused and often extremely complicated glass structure contrasting noticeably with the thin and sharply defined casing of lined glass. The latter type became popular from the fourteenth century onward, employing a variety of colors (often in combination), while earlier flashed examples from the twelfth and thirteenth centuries are found most frequently, but not exclusively, in the reds. Connick believed that this colour was the first to be treated in this manner—richly saturated reds of some formulas having a tendency to appear dark or opaque—hence this 'clever expedient' to preserve both the richness and brilliance of the color. C. J. Connick, *Adventures in Light and Color*, New York, 1937, p. 256.
4. G. Chesneau, 'Contribution à l'étude chimiques des vitraux du moyen-âge,' *Comptes rendus*, Académie des Sciences, Paris, CLX, 1915, pp. 622–624; also 'Contribution à l'étude de la technique des vitraux du moyen-âge,' *Bulletin monumental*, Paris, XCII, 1933, pp. 265–295.
5. Henry John Tress, 'Periodic Bands in Ruby Glasses,' *Journal of the Society of Glass Technology*, XXXVIII, 1954, 35n–37n. Dr. Charles D. Spencer of General Electric Corporation's Research Laboratories has kindly brought my attention to this article.
6. Opinion is divided with respect to exterior patina on old stained glass. Traditionally, it has been regarded as the natural result of centuries of weathering, during which time the rain, changing temperatures, sunlight, organic and inorganic particles in the air, have all acted upon the surfaces of the glass to deposit the coating and cause the pits and other decomposition found there. Recently I have asked chemists to analyze the surfaces of the few twelfth-century fragments in my possession, and conflicting testimony has arisen. Working from the same material, one chemist reports that he had found traces of litharge (an early form of putty) on these surfaces, suggesting that it was spread on the glass when it was new to enhance its translucency, but another chemist can find no evidence of litharge, and contends that the patina is caused by strains within the glass and prolonged reaction of the vitreous material with the elements. Chevreul concluded that this *matière grumelée* was nothing but '*du vieux mastic de vitrier formé d'huile siccative et de craie.*' Later, he says that '*je pense que la plus grande partie provenait de l'atmosphère.*' (M. E. Chevreul, 'Chimie appliquée aux beaux-arts—mémoire sur les vitraux peints,' *Comptes rendus*, Académie des Sciences, LVII, Paris, 1863, pp. 655–666.) This is still an unresolved question, requiring extensive study by properly equipped investigators who have access to a large amount of material.

Fortuitous or not, there is no doubt that the exterior surfacing of old glass has enhanced and enriched its effect (when it has not blackened the colors altogether), for the pits and deposits scattered unevenly over the panels offer additional resistance to the light, halting it in some places and in other areas allowing bright gleams to shine through. This coating, therefore, along with the inner complications of the glass, contributes to the vibrancy of the older medium.

7. References to jewels have occasionally given rise to literal interpretations, e.g., that medieval windows contain crushed particles of sapphires or other precious stones, a notion unsubstantiated by chemical analysis, which has shown that metallic oxides are the chief colorants. See Chesneau, *op cit.*, CLX, 1915, pp. 622–624. Cobalt is used for blue glass, and iron and copper for red, as a rule. Thus far I have not encountered any analysis which detects gold as a colorant for red stained glass of the twelfth and thirteenth centuries, although gold has been used extensively for this purpose in subsequent periods and in modern times, possessing exceptional coloring powers, for one part of gold will impart a vivid ruby-red hue to 10,000 parts of glass. Max Bauer, *Edelsteinkunde*, Leipzig, 1932, p. 824. The notion of gold in medieval glass, however, was apparently quite prevalent in the eighteenth century, for it is recorded that during the French Revolution the Convention Nationale, needing money, proposed to melt the windows in the churches to extract gold from the red glass. A chemist named Darcet was ordered to determine the quantity of gold in these windows, but in submitting his analysis he disappointed everyone by stating that he found no gold but only small amounts of copper and iron as colorants. See L. Ottin, *Le vitrail*, Paris, H. Laurens, 1896, p. 353. Ottin thinks that this belief in the presence of gold (when not disproved) was one reason for the destruction of so many ancient windows.

8. Jean Escard, *Les pierres précieuses*, Paris, 1914, Plate XXIII.

9. *Ibid.*, pp. 312–323; 445–459. Jewelers distinguish between 'artificial' gems, which approximate the natural properties of real stones, and 'imitation' gems, which are of a lower order, made from lesser materials. See the article 'Artificial Gems' in the *Encyclopaedia Britannica*, 11th Ed., XI, pp. 569–572.

10. Max Bauer, *Edelsteinkunde*, *op. cit.*, pp. 822–824.

11. Thomas Nicols, *Arcula Gemmea, or A Cabinet of Jewels*, London, 1653, p. 55. A century earlier, Benvenuto Cellini made similar observations in *Due Trattati*, Florence, 1568.

12. Nicols, *op. cit.*, p. 19.

13. This work was later enlarged by Christopher Merret and Johann Kunckel, becoming a standard international reference on glass technology and enjoying many editions. I have used the French edition, *Art de la verrerie*, Paris, 1752. See esp. Book IV, pp. 167–170; Book V, pp. 173ff.

14. Noel Heaton, 'The Production and Identification of Artificial Precious Stones,' *Annual Report of the Smithsonian Institution*, Washington, D.C., 1911, pp. 217–234.

15. M. P. E. Berthelot, *Histoire des sciences. La chimie au moyen âge*, Paris, 1893, pp. 5ff. For an account of the complicated relationships between these texts, see R. P. Johnson, 'The *Compositiones Variae*

from Codex 490, Biblioteca Capitolare, Lucca, Italy. An Introductory Study,' *Illinois Studies in Language and Literature*, XX, 3, Urbana, 1939. Many passages in Theophilus and Heraclius, for example, can be traced to Classical sources, transmitted during the early Christian period through such works as the *Etymologiae* of Isidore of Seville.

16. Other traces of antiquity are found in the frequent appearance of antique engraved gems and cameos on medieval objects. See W. S. Heckscher, 'Relics of Pagan Antiquity in Medieval Settings,' *Journal of the Warburg Institute*, I, 3, 1937, pp. 204–220. Dr. Hanns Swarzenski has kindly brought this important article to my attention.

17. Tr. Robert Hendrie, London, 1847. A new English edition and translation has been made by J. Hawthorne and C. Smith, University of Chicago Press, 1963.

18. In *Quellenschriften für Kunstgeschichte und Kunsttechnik des Mittelalters*, IV, ed. Albert Ilg, Vienna, 1888. I wish to thank Mrs. Irene Heppner of The Cleveland Museum of Art for assistance in the translation of this work.

19. This analogy is strengthened when we learn in James Barrelet's authoritative *La verrerie en France*, Paris, 1953 (see pp. 20, 33, 39–43), that glass cabochons and plaques were used to decorate the walls of Romanesque and Gothic churches. I am indebted to Mr. Paul Norman Perrot of the Corning Glass Center for this reference.

Louis Grodecki, in the Catalogue for the exhibition, *Vitraux de France*, Paris, 1953, says on page 27: '*La beauté des vitraux est tout d'abord la beauté de la matière qui les constitue, du verre, cette pierre précieuse artificielle, de la monture métallique qui le maintient et l'enchâsse.*'

20. See esp. Édgar de Bruyne, *Études d'esthétique médiévale*, Bruges, 1946, 3 vols.

21. Escard, *op. cit.*, p. 21.

22. *Ibid.*, p. 20.

23. Recently, through the courtesy of Dr. James J. Rorimer and Mr. William H. Forsyth of the Metropolitan Museum of Art, I have been able to examine some of the glass gems in their medieval collections. Our search was necessarily limited to chipped and fractured pieces which could be examined for internal structure, but already the findings have been promising, for a lined ruby was discovered among the gems of a twelfth-century German crucifix, and random striations of vitreous reds were found within the body of a St. Christopher medallion dating from the Romanesque period.

24. Tr. Erwin Panofsky, *Abbot Suger on the Abbey Church of Saint-Denis*, Princeton, 1940.

25. *Ibid.*, pp. 109–113.

26. This can be observed in both old and modern pieces. I am indebted to M. Jean Lafond of Paris for allowing me to inspect many examples in his extensive collection.

27. Of the *filets ornementaux* in windows, Louis Grodecki says: '*On peut dire que le rôle de cette couleur n'est plus, dans les verrières basses, d'augmenter la clarté du vitrail, mais simplement d'aider à sa lisibilité décorative, de saupoudrer, en quelque sorte, de petites taches de lumière pure, d'une multitude de petits points scintillants, les surfaces saturées de couleur vive.*' 'Le vitrail et l'architecture au XIIe et au XIIIe siècles,' *Gazette des Beaux-Arts*, II, 1949, p. 13.

28. *Traité des couleurs pour la peinture en émail*, Paris, 1765.
29. *Ibid.*, p. 222.
30. *Ibid.*, p. 217.

NOTES TO CHAPTER FOUR

1. In making these distinctions I am using terms which Professor Meyer Schapiro has applied in his Columbia University lectures on medieval sculpture.
2. Karl Young, *The Drama of the Mediaeval Church*, Oxford, 1933, *passim*.
3. The idea of the *Corpus Verum* is also an important part of the program for the sculptures of the *Royal Portal*. Adolf Katzenellenbogen, *The Sculptural Programs of Chartres Cathedral*, Baltimore, 1959, pp. 7–24.
4. This panel has been extensively restored, but in my opinion it is an excellent restoration, with the exception of the faces of the Three Kings.
5. Henri Jougla de Morenas, *Grand armorial de France*, Paris, 1934, 6 vols.; see esp. Vol. I, 1–21. Also, Abbé Auber, *Histoire et théorie du symbolisme religieuse*, Paris, 1871, II, pp. 545–548; Henri Gourdon de Genouillac, *L'art héraldique*, Paris, 1889, p. 19. See also the article 'Blason' in *Noveau larousse illustré*, II, 1922, p. 110.

BIBLIOGRAPHY

STAINED GLASS

Corpus Vitrearum Medii Aevi, Comité International d'Histoire de l'Art; Union Académique International. (Vols. according to country.) 1956 forward.

Arnold, Hugh, *Stained Glass*, London, 1913.

Aubert, Marcel, *Le vitrail en France*, Paris, 1946.

Aubert, Marcel, Chastel, A., Grodecki, L. *et al, Le vitrail français*, Paris, 1958.

Aubert, Marcel, *Vitraux des cathédrales de France*, Paris, 1937.

Connick, Charles, J., *Adventures in Light and Color*, New York, 1937.

Day, Lewis, F., *Windows, A Book about Stained and Painted Glass*, London, 1902.

Delaporte, Y., and Houvet, E., *Les vitraux de la cathédrale de Chartres*, Chartres, 1926, 4 vols.

Frankl, Paul, 'The Chronology of the Stained Glass in Chartres Cathedral,' *Art Bulletin*, XLV, 1963, pp. 301–322.

Grodecki, L., *Les vitraux des églises de France*, Paris, 1948.

Grodecki, L., *Vitraux de France*, Paris, 1953.

Grodecki, L., 'Le vitrail et l'architecture au XIIIᵉ et au XIIIᵉ siècles,' *Gazette des Beaux-arts*, II, 1949, pp. 5–24.

Johnson, J. R. 'The Tree of Jesse Window of Chartres,' *Speculum*, XXXVI, 1961, pp. 1–22.

Lasteyrie, F. de, *Histoire de la peinture sur verre*, Paris, 1857, 2 vols.

Lévy, Edmond, and Capronnier, J., *Histoire de la peinture sur verre*, Brussels, 1860.

Magne, Lucien, *L'Œuvre des peintres verriers français*, Paris, 1885.

Mâle, Emile, 'La peinture sur verre en France,' in *Histoire générale de l'art*, Paris, 1905, I, II and IV.

Martin, A., and Cahier, C., *Monographie de la cathédrale de Bourges*, Paris, 1841–44, 2 vols.

Oidtmann, Heinrich, *Die Glasmalerei*, Cologne, 1893–1898, 2 vols.

Ottin, L., *Le vitrail*, Paris, 1896.

Schmarsow, A., *Kompositionsgesetze romanischer Glasgemälde*, Leipzig, 1916.

Sowers, R., *The Lost Art, A Survey of One Thousand Years of Stained Glass*, New York, 1954.

Viollet-le-Duc, E., 'Vitrail,' in *Dictionnaire raisonné de l'architecture française* (9 vols.), Paris, 1854–68, IX, pp. 373–462. Translated into English by Francis Palmer Smith, *Mediaeval Stained Glass*, Atlanta, Georgia, 1942.

Wentzel, H., *Meisterwerke der Glasmalerei*, Berlin, 1951.

Westlake, N. H. J., *A History of Design in Stained and Painted Glass*, London, 1881–94, 4 vols.

CHARTRES CATHEDRAL

Adams, Henry, *Mont-Saint-Michel and Chartres*, Boston, 1905.

Aubert, Marcel, *La cathédrale de Chartres*, Paris, 1952.

Bulteau, l'Abbé, *Monographie de la cathédrale de Chartres*, 3 vols., Chartres, 1887.

Grodecki, L., *Chartres*, New York, 1963.

Durand, Paul, *Monographie de Notre-Dame de Chartres*, Paris, 1867–81.

Houvet, E., *Monographie de la cathédrale de Chartres*, Chartres, 1930.

Katzenellenbogen, A., *The Sculptural Programs of Chartres Cathedral*, Baltimore, 1958.

Lassus, J. B., *Monographie de la cathédrale de Chartres*, Paris, 1842.

Mâle, Emile, *Nôtre Dame de Chartres*, Paris, 1948.

Simson, Otto von, *The Gothic Cathedral*, New York, 1956.

SCIENTIFIC INVESTIGATION OF GLASS

Barrelet, James, *La verrière en France*, Paris, 1953.

Berthelot, M. P. E., *Histoire des sciences, et la chimie au moyen-âge*, Paris, 1893, 3 vols.

Bontemps, G., *Guide du verrier*, Paris, 1868.

Chesneau, G., 'Contribution à l'étude chimique des vitraux du moyen-âge,' *Comptes rendus*, CLX, 1915, pp. 622–624.

Chesneau, G., 'Contribution à l'étude de la technique des vitraux du moyen-âge,' *Bulletin monumental*, XLII, 1933, pp. 265–295.

Chevreul, M. E., 'Chimie appliquée aux beaux-arts. Mémoire sur les vitraux peints,' *Comptes rendus*, LVII, 1863, pp. 655–666.

Gruber, J. J., in Aubert *et al.*, *Le vitrail français*, Paris, 1958.

Heaton, Noel, 'The Production and Identification of Artificial Precious Stones,' *Annual Report of the Smithsonian Institution*, 1911, pp. 217–234.

Singer, Charles (ed.), *A History of Technology*, Oxford, 1956, II.

Tress, Henry John, 'Periodic Bands in Ruby Glasses,' *Journal of the Society of Glass Technology*, XXXVIII, 1954, pp. 35–37.

COLOR AND COLOR THEORY

Aristotle, *Works*, W. D. Ross (ed.), Oxford, 1930. *Meteorologica*, III, I–4; *De Anima*, II, 7; *De Somnis*, II, 459.

British Colour Council, *Dictionary of Colour Standards*, London, 1951.

Chevreul, M. E., *De la loi du contraste simultané des couleurs*, Paris, 1839.

Committee on Colorimetry, *The Science of Color*, New York, 1953.

Evans, Ralph M., *An Introduction to Color*, New York, 1948.

Field, George, *Chromatics*, London, 1817.

Galileo, *Opere*, Bologna, 1656.

Goethe, J., *Farbenlehre*, Munich, 1810. Tr. Chas. Eastlake, *Theory of Colours*, London, 1840.

Hartridge, H., *Recent Advances in the Physiology of Vision*, London, 1950.

Helmholtz, H. von, *Physiological Optics*, ed. Southall, New York, 1924.

Jones, Owen, *The Grammar of Ornament*, London, 1856.

Jones, Owen, *Lectures on Architecture and the Decorative Arts*, London, 1863.

Katz, David, *The World of Colour*, London, 1935.

Wilkinson, John, *On Colour and on the Necessity for a General Diffusion of Taste Among all Classes*, London, 1858.

Willmer, E. N., *Retinal Structure and Colour Vision*, Cambridge, 1946.

Wright, W. D., *The Measurement of Colour*, London, 1944.

Wright, W. D., *The Perception of Light*, London, 1938.

GENERAL

Bruyne, Edgar de, *Études d'esthétique médiévale*, Bruges, 1946, 3 vols.

Panofsky, Erwin, *Abbot Suger on the Abbey Church of St-Denis*, Princeton, 1946.

Pliny, *Natural History*, tr. Bostock, London, 1858.

Saint-Paul, Anthyme, *Viollet-le-Duc*, Paris, 1881.

Schapiro, Meyer, 'On the Esthetic Attitude in Romanesque Art,' in *Art and Thought*, K. Iyer (ed.), London, 1947.

Schapiro, Meyer, 'From Mozarabic to Romanesque in Silos,' *Art Bulletin*, XXI, 1940, pp. 312–374.

Schöne, Wolfgang, *Über das Licht in der Malerei*, Berlin, 1954.

Sturrock, W., and Staley, K., *Fundamentals of Light and Lighting*, Cleveland, 1953.

Theophilus (Rugerus), *Diversarum Artium Schedula*, tr. Robert Hendrie, London, 1847; Hawthorne and Smith, University of Chicago, 1963.

INDEX

Angers, Cathedral, 7
Aristotle, 17
ascensio, 24
Aubert, M., 28

beading, 36, 65, 67
Bontemps, G., 12
Bourges, Cathedral, 7
Brücke, E., 44–45

cabochon, gems, 61, 63
Canterbury, Cathedral, 7
carbuncle, 59
Celestial Jerusalem, 63
Chartres, *passim*
  fenestration, 7
  interior light, 10, 15, 16, 18–25,
    29
  restoration of windows, 26–27
  visibility of glass, 7, 12, 29
Chesneau, G., 55–57
Chevreul, M., 45–46
color
  choice and composition, 67–79
  irradiation, 29–31
  perception, 16–21
  translucent, 29
color photography, 33–34
Compositiones ad tingenda, 60
Connick, C., 24, 64
Corpus Verum, 68

Day, L., 44
Delaporte, Yves, 33
détente, sculpture, 24
doublet, 59
Durand, P., 33

enframement of scenes, 67
Escard, J., 58

eye, the human
  accommodation range, 15, 16
  dark adaptation, 11, 17
  fatigue, 22–23
  mesopic vision, 18–21
  perception of light and colour,
    9–15
  phenomenon of decay, 51
  photopic and scotopic vision, 17,
    20
  variations in acuity, 20–22

Field, G., 47

Galileo, G., 42–43
gems, imitation, 57–66, 74
glare, 9, 10, 12–15
glass
  analysis of fragments, 52, 64
  "antique", 54
  flashed, 54–55, 54 n
  inner structure, 53–57
  lined, 54
  microscopic studies, 53–55
  patina, 53, 57 n
  "ruby", 53–57
Griffin, D., 22
grisaille, 9
Grodecki, L., 12 n, 16, 28

Hartridge, H., 14
hatching, 36
Hayward, J., 55
Heckscher, W. S., 60 n.
Helmholtz, H. von., 16, 42–43, 45
Heraclius, 61–62
heraldry, 66, 74
Houvet, Étienne, 33

jewelry, medieval, 57–66

Jones, Owen, 48–50

Katz, D., 22

La Belle Verrière, Nôtre Dame de, 39
Lapidaire of Marbode, 76
light
  irradiation, 14, 29, 43
  measurement, 10
  perception, 17
  reflected, 12–14
  sensitivity, 16, 17
  symbolism, 4
  translucent, 12–14

Mappae Clavicula, 60
Marbode, Bishop of Rennes, 76
Milan, Cathedral altar, 65
Mohs scale, 60
Montamy, D. de, 65
mosaics, 9

Neri, A., 59
Nicols, T., 59
Nôtre Dame de la Belle Verrière, 39
Nôtre Dame de Paris, 37

Oidtmann, H., 40

painting, on glass, 36, 53
Panofsky, Erwin, 24 n, 78
Plateau, J., 42–43
Pliny, the Elder, 60
Poitiers, 7
Portinari altarpiece, 75
precious stones, imitation, 57–66
Pugin, A. W. N., 26
Purkinje, J., 17

Purkinje "shift", 16–17, 51

radiantia, 4
Rose of France, 8
Royal Portal, Chartres, 75

Saint, Lawrence, 56
Saint-Denis, Abbey Church, 27
Saint-Paul, A., 46–47
Saint-Rémi, Reims, 37–38
Sainte Chapelle, Paris, 8
Schapiro, M., 51 n, 68 n
Schedula Diversarum Artium, 60
Schöne, W., 57
Sens, 7
Simon, Ellen, 31 n
Sowers, R., 28, 28 n.
stained glass, *passim*
  Baroque, 15
  damage to, 10
  destruction of, 8
  Renaissance, 14, 23, 78
  resetting after wars, 8
  Rococo, 15
Suger, Abbot, 24, 63–64
surface gloss, 9
surface light, 8

Theophilus, called Rugerus, 28, 60–61
Tree of Jesse window, 40–41
Tress, H., 56
twilight vision, 16, 17

Verrier, J., 28
Viollet-le-Duc, E., 26–52

Wald, G., 22
Wilkinson, J., 50

Young, K., 68

COLUMBIA UNIVERSITY STUDIES
IN ART HISTORY AND ARCHAEOLOGY

Other titles will be announced as ready

ARCHITECTURAL PRINCIPLES IN
THE AGE OF HUMANISM

by Rudolf Wittkower

CITY PLANNING

by Camillo Sitte
Translated by George R. Collins
and Christiane Craseman Collins

CAMILLO SITTE AND THE BIRTH
OF MODERN CITY PLANNING

by George R. Collins
and Christiane Craseman Collins

THE RADIANCE OF CHARTRES

by James Rosser Johnson

THE CHICAGO SCHOOL OF ARCHITECTURE

by Mark L. Peisch